madison r

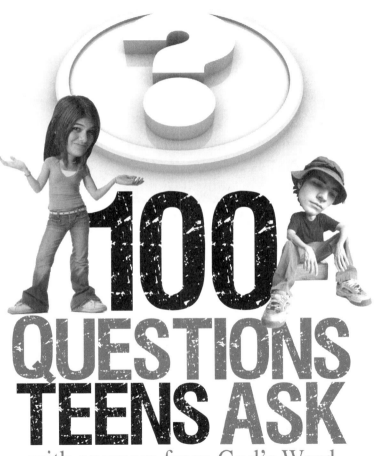

100 QUESTIONS TEENS ASK

with answers from God's Word

FAMILY
Christian Stores®

Scripture quotations are taken from:

The Holy Bible, King James Version (KJV)

The Holy Bible, New International Version (NIV) Copyright © 1973, 1978, 1984, by International Bible Society. Used by permission of Zondervan Publishing House. All rights reserved.

The Holy Bible, New King James Version (NKJV) Copyright © 1982 by Thomas Nelson, Inc. Used by permission.

Holy Bible, New Living Translation, (NLT) copyright © 1996. Used by permission of Tyndale House Publishers, Inc., Wheaton, Illinois 60189. All rights reserved.

The Message (MSG)- This edition issued by contractual arrangement with NavPress, a division of The Navigators, U.S.A. Originally published by NavPress in English as THE MESSAGE: The Bible in Contemporary Language copyright 2002-2003 by Eugene Peterson. All rights reserved.

New Century Version®. (NCV) Copyright © 1987, 1988, 1991 by Word Publishing, a division of Thomas Nelson, Inc. All rights reserved. Used by permission.

The New American Standard Bible®, (NASB) Copyright © 1960, 1962, 1963, 1968, 1971, 1972, 1973, 1975, 1977, 1995 by The Lockman Foundation. Used by permission.

International Children's Bible®, New Century Version®. (ICB) Copyright © 1986, 1988, 1999 by Tommy Nelson™, a division of Thomas Nelson, Inc. All rights reserved. Used by permission.

The Holman Christian Standard Bible™ (HCSB) Copyright © 1999, 2000, 2001 by Holman Bible Publishers. Used by permission.

Cover Design Kim Russell / Wahoo Designs

Page Layout by Bart Dawson

ISBN 978-1-58334-008-0

Printed in the United States of America

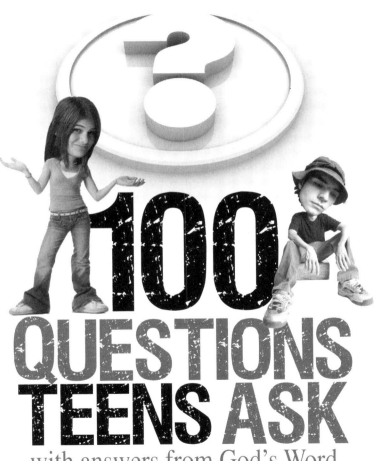

100 QUESTIONS TEENS ASK

with answers from God's Word

INDEX OF TOPICS

Introduction

Okay, when you've got questions, where do you turn for answers: Your friends? Your parents? Dr. Phil? All of the above? Well, there's a better source of wisdom, and it's probably taking up space on your bookshelf. That source of wisdom, of course, is the Holy Bible.

This book contains 100 questions that teens (like you) ask, along with answers based upon truths contained in God's Holy Word.

Being a young adult in today's world isn't easy. Your world is filled with distractions and temptations that were unknown to previous generations. And the world is changing so rapidly that, at times, it seems difficult to catch your breath and keep your balance.

In a rapidly changing world, God remains unchanged. In a society that is built upon the shifting sands of popular culture, God's laws remain constant. In a time of uncertainty and doubt, God's promises are sure and true. This book addresses topics of profound importance to young adults. Each brief chapter of this text is intended to help you build—and rebuild—your faith.

This book is intended to reassure you of the eternal promises that are found in God's Holy Word and of God's never-ending love for you. May these pages help you answer the most important questions you face, and may you, in turn, share your answers with the friends and family members whom God has seen fit to place along your path.

QUESTION 1

NIV: "I wish that all men were as I am. But each man has his own gift from God; one has this gift, another has that.

Sure, I have abilities. But what should I do about the abilities and opportunities God has given me?

THE QUICK ANSWER

God has given you abilities and opportunities. Discover those abilities and develop them. The Lord has work for you to do . . . now!

Making the Most of Your Abilities

Each one has his own gift from God,
one in this manner and another in that.
1 Corinthians 7:7 NKJV

God knew precisely what He was doing when He gave you a unique set of abilities and opportunities. And now, God wants you to use those talents for the glory of His kingdom. So here's the big question: will you choose to use your talents, or not?

Your Heavenly Father wants you to be a faithful steward of the gifts He has given you. But you live in a society that may encourage you to do otherwise. You face countless temptations to squander your time, your resources, and your talents. So you must be keenly aware of the inevitable distractions that can waste your time, your energy, and your opportunities.

100 QUESTIONS TEENS ASK

God has blessed you with many opportunities to serve Him, and He has given you every tool you need to do so. Today, accept this challenge: value the talent that God has given you, nourish it, make it grow, and share it with the world, beginning now.

You are the only person on earth who can use your ability.

Zig Ziglar

It is not my ability, but my response to God's ability, that counts.

Corrie ten Boom

Natural abilities are like natural plants; they need pruning by study.

Francis Bacon

These are gifts from God arranged by infinite wisdom, notes that make up the scores of creation's loftiest symphony, threads that compose the master tapestry of the universe.

A. W. Tozer

When we've done what we can—God will do what we can't!

Anonymous

*God has given everyone their own ability. Use your ability to help others grow closer to God!

QUESTION 2

As a Christian, should I expect to receive God's abundance, or not?

THE QUICK ANSWER

God will provide for your needs if you stay focused on doing His will.

God's Abundance

*The master was full of praise. "Well done, my good
and faithful servant. You have been faithful in handling this small
amount, so now I will give you many more responsibilities.
Let's celebrate together!"*
Matthew 25:21 NLT

God sent His Son so that mankind might enjoy the abundant life that Jesus describes in the familiar words of John 10:10. But, God's gifts are not guaranteed; they must be claimed by those who choose to follow Christ. As you make plans for life, you may be asking yourself, "What kind of life does God intend for me?" The answer can be found in God's promise of abundance: those who accept that promise and live according to God's commandments are eternally blessed.

Whether or not we accept God's abundance is, of course, up to each of us. When we entrust our hearts and our days to the One who created us, we experience God's peace through the grace and sacrifice of His Son. But, when we turn our thoughts and our energies away from God's commandments, we inevitably forfeit the earthly peace and spiritual abundance that might otherwise be ours.

What is your focus today? Are you focused on God's Word and His will for your life? Or are you focused on the distractions of a difficult, temptation-filled world? If you sincerely seek the spiritual abundance that your Savior offers, then you should follow Him completely and without reservation. When you do, you will receive the love, the life, and the abundance that He has promised.

———————————

The only way you can experience abundant life is to surrender your plans to Him.

Charles Stanley

It would be wrong to have a "poverty complex," for to think ourselves paupers is to deny either the King's riches or to deny our being His children.

Catherine Marshall

God's riches are beyond anything we could ask or even dare to imagine! If my life gets gooey and stale, I have no excuse.

Barbara Johnson

What does the Bible say about the kind of relationship that I should establish with Jesus Christ?

THE QUICK ANSWER

It is critically important to be certain that you have welcomed Christ into your heart. If you've accepted Christ, congratulations. If not, the time to accept Him is now!

Accepting Christ

For the wages of sin is death, but the gift of God is eternal life in Christ Jesus our Lord.
Romans 6:23 HCSB

Sometimes, we must accept life on its terms, not our own. Life has a way of unfolding, not as we will, but as it will. And sometimes, there is precious little we can do to change things.

When events transpire that are beyond our control, we have a choice: we can either learn the art of acceptance, or we can make ourselves miserable as we struggle to change the unchangeable.

We must entrust the things we cannot change to God. Once we have done so, we can prayerfully and faithfully tackle the important work that He has placed before us: the things we can change.

It's your heart that Jesus longs for: your will to be made His own with self on the cross forever, and Jesus alone on the throne.

Ruth Bell Graham

A man can accept what Christ has done without knowing how it works; indeed, he certainly won't know how it works until he's accepted it.

C. S. Lewis

Choose Jesus Christ! Deny yourself, take up the Cross, and follow Him—for the world must be shown. The world must see, in us, a discernible, visible, startling difference.

Elisabeth Elliot

The most profound essence of my nature is that I am capable of receiving God.

St. Augustine

QUESTION 4

I know that addiction is a big problem. Does the Bible have anything to say about it?

THE QUICK ANSWER

If you can't seem to get a handle on your appetites, the time to address your problem is today, not tomorrow. Gather your courage and pay a visit to your pastor, to a counselor, or to a local 12-step group. Help is waiting, but you'll need to ask for it. So ask.

Beware of Addiction!

But prove yourselves doers of the word, and not merely hearers.
James 1:22 NASB

Ours is a society that glamorizes the use of drugs, alcohol, cigarettes, and other addictive substances. Why? The answer can be summed up in one word: money. Simply put, addictive substances are big money makers, so suppliers (of both legal and illegal substances) work overtime to make certain that people like you sample their products. The suppliers need a steady stream of new customers because the old ones are dying off (fast), so they engage in a no-holds-barred struggle to find new users—or more accurately, new abusers.

If you want to wreck your self-esteem—not to mention your health—allow yourself to become an addict. But if you want to enhance your sense of self-worth, treat addictive substances like life-destroying poisons that they are.

God cannot build character without our cooperation. If we resist Him, then He chastens us into submission. But, if we submit to Him, then He can accomplish His work. He is not satisfied with a halfway job. God wants a perfect work; He wants a finished product that is mature and complete.

Warren Wiersbe

A man may not be responsible for his last drink, but he certainly was for the first.

Billy Graham

I abstain myself from alcoholic drink in every form, and I think that others would be wise to do the same.

C. H. Spurgeon

One reason I'm a teetotaler is that I got so disgusted being mistreated due to a man's drinking to excess that I never have wanted to run the risk of mistreating my own family by drinking.

Jerry Clower

Sometimes, I've got a pretty short fuse, and it's easy for me to become upset. What does the Bible say about anger?

THE QUICK ANSWER

Time Out! If you become angry, the time to step away from the situation is before you say unkind words or do unkind things—not after. It's perfectly okay to place yourself in "time out" until you can calm down.

Beyond Anger

A patient person [shows] great understanding,
but a quick-tempered one promotes foolishness.
Proverbs 14:29 HCSB

Temper tantrums are usually unproductive, unattractive, unforgettable, and unnecessary. Perhaps that's why Proverbs 16:32 states that, "Controlling your temper is better than capturing a city" (NCV).

If you've allowed anger to become a regular visitor at your house, today you must pray for wisdom, for patience, and for a heart that is so filled with love and forgiveness that it contains no room for bitterness. God will help you terminate your tantrums if you ask Him to. And God can help you perfect your ability to be patient if you ask Him to. So ask Him, and then wait patiently for the ever-more-patient you to arrive.

When you strike out in anger, you may miss the other person, but you will always hit yourself.

Jim Gallery

Anger is the noise of the soul; the unseen irritant of the heart; the relentless invader of silence.

Max Lucado

When something robs you of your peace of mind, ask yourself if it is worth the energy you are expending on it. If not, then put it out of your mind in an act of discipline. Every time the thought of "it" returns, refuse it.

Kay Arthur

The only justifiable anger defends the great, glorious, and holy nature of our God.

John MacArthur

Anger breeds remorse in the heart, discord in the home, bitterness in the community, and confusion in the state.

Billy Graham

QUESTION 6

Should I be afraid to ask God for the things I really want?

THE QUICK ANSWER

If you need something, ask. And remember this: God is listening, and He wants to hear from you right now.

Asking God

So I say to you, ask, and it will be given to you; seek,
and you will find; knock, and it will be opened to you.
For everyone who asks receives, and he who seeks finds,
and to him who knocks it will be opened.
Luke 11:9-10 NKJV

Is God hanging out at the far end of the universe, too far away to hear your requests? Nope, God is right here, right now, waiting to hear from you. Are you ready to talk to Him? Hopefully, you've learned the wisdom of asking God for His help.

Are you in need? Ask God to sustain you. Are you troubled? Take your worries to Him, and He will comfort you. Are you weary? Seek God's strength. Do you have questions about your future that you simply can't answer? Ask your Heavenly Father for insight and direction. In all things great and small, seek

God's wisdom and His will. He will hear your prayers, and He will answer.

When will we realize that we're not troubling God with our questions and concerns? His heart is open to hear us—his touch nearer than our next thought—as if no one in the world existed but us. Our very personal God wants to hear from us personally.

Gigi Graham Tchividjian

All we have to do is to acknowledge our need, move from self-sufficiency to dependence, and ask God to become our hiding place.

Bill Hybels

Some people think God does not like to be troubled with our constant asking. But, the way to trouble God is not to come at all.

D. L. Moody

Don't be afraid to ask your Heavenly Father for anything you need. Indeed, nothing is too small for God's attention or too great for his power.

Dennis Swanberg

What kind of attitude is best for me and my friends?

THE QUICK ANSWER

Learn about Jesus and His attitude. Then try and do what Jesus would do.

The Right Kind of Attitude

There is one thing I always do. Forgetting the past and straining
toward what is ahead, I keep trying to reach the goal
and get the prize for which God called me . . . .
Philippians 3:13–14 NCV

Now that you're growing older and becoming more mature, it's time to make plans for the next leg of your life's journey: becoming an adult. And as you make plans, remember that the quality of that journey will depend, in part, on the quality of your thoughts. If you allow yourself to fall into the unfortunate habit of negative thinking, you will bring needless suffering into your life. But if you choose, instead, to follow the directive of Philippians 4:8, you will focus your attention upon "whatsoever things are true . . . honest . . . just . . . pure . . . lovely . . . and of good report." And when you do, your life will be richer for it.

100 QUESTIONS TEENS ASK

I became aware of one very important concept I had missed before: my attitude—not my circumstances—was what was making me unhappy.

Vonette Bright

A positive attitude will have positive results because attitudes are contagious.

Zig Ziglar

The people whom I have seen succeed best in life have always been cheerful and hopeful people who went about their business with a smile on their faces.

Charles Kingsley

If you can't tell whether your glass is half-empty of half-full, you don't need another glass; what you need is better eyesight . . . and a more thankful heart.

Marie T. Freeman

Life is 10% what happens to you and 90% how you respond to it.

Charles Swindoll

How does God want me and my friends to behave?

THE QUICK ANSWER

If you're not sure that it's the right thing to do, don't do it! And if you're not sure that it's the truth, don't tell it.

Following the Right Path

Don't be deceived: God is not mocked.
For whatever a man sows he will also reap, because the one
who sows to his flesh will reap corruption from the flesh,
but the one who sows to the Spirit will reap
eternal life from the Spirit.
Galatians 6:7-8 HCSB

Okay, answer these questions honestly: Do you behave differently because of your relationship with Jesus? Do you have a better attitude? And do you see the world in a different way? Or do you see things (and do things) in pretty much the same way that you would if you weren't a believer? Hopefully, the fact that you've invited Christ to reign over your heart means that you've made BIG changes in your thoughts and your actions.

Doing the right thing is not always easy, especially when you're tired or frustrated. But, doing the wrong thing almost always leads to trouble. And sometimes, it leads to BIG trouble.

If you're determined to follow "the crowd," you may soon find yourself headed in the wrong direction. So here's some advice: Don't follow the crowd—follow Jesus. And keep following Him every day of your life, beginning with this day.

We are to leave an impression on all those we meet that communicates whose we are and what kingdom we represent.

Lisa Bevere

Christians are the citizens of heaven, and while we are on earth, we ought to behave like heaven's citizens.

Warren Wiersbe

Life is a series of choices between the bad, the good, and the best. Everything depends on how we choose.

Vance Havner

Order your soul; reduce your wants; associate in Christian community; obey the laws; trust in Providence.

St. Augustine

He leads us in the paths of righteousness wherever we are placed.

Oswald Chambers

Is the Bible really God's Word, or is it simply another book?

THE QUICK ANSWER

The Bible is the best-selling book of all time . . . for good reason. Ruth Bell Graham, wife of evangelist Billy Graham, believed in the importance of God's Word: "The Reference Point for the Christian is the Bible. All values, judgments, and attitudes must be gauged in relationship to this Reference Point." Make certain that you're an avid reader of God's best-seller, and make sure that you keep reading it as long as you live!

Nourished by the Word

*Blessed are those who hunger and thirst for righteousness,
for they will be filled.*
Matthew 5:6 NIV

If you're serious about really getting to know God better, then you'll need to get really serious about reading your Bible every day (not just on Sundays!).

The Bible is unlike any other book. It is a priceless gift from your Creator, a tool that God intends for you to use in every aspect of your life. And, it contains promises upon which you, as a Christian, can and must depend.

D. L. Moody observed, "The Bible was not given to increase our knowledge but to change our lives." God's Holy Word is, indeed, a life-changing, one-of-a-kind treasure. Handle it with care, but more importantly, handle it every day.

Nobody ever outgrows Scripture; the book widens and deepens with our years.

C. H. Spurgeon

I study the Bible as I gather apples. First, I shake the whole tree that the ripest might fall. Then I shake each limb; I shake each branch and every twig. Then, I look under every leaf.

Martin Luther

Study the Bible and observe how the persons behaved and how God dealt with them. There is explicit teaching on every condition of life.

Corrie ten Boom

Reading news without reading the Bible will inevitably lead to an unbalanced life, an anxious spirit, a worried and depressed soul.

Bill Bright

How does God want me to treat my body?

THE QUICK ANSWER

God needs you. Take care of the body He has given you.

Taking Care of Your Body

For we know that if our earthly house, a tent, is destroyed,
we have a building from God, a house not made with hands,
eternal in the heavens.

2 Corinthians 5:1 HCSB

How do you treat your body? Do you treat it with the reverence and respect it deserves, or do you take it more or less for granted? Well, the Bible has clear instructions about the way you should take care of the miraculous body that God has given you.

God's Word teaches us that our bodies are "temples" that belong to God (1 Corinthians 6:19-20). We are commanded (not encouraged, not advised—we are commanded!) to treat our bodies with respect and honor. We do so by making wise choices and by making those choices consistently over an extended period of time.

Do you sincerely seek to improve the overall quality of your life and your health? Then promise yourself—and God—that you will begin making the kind of wise choices that will lead to a longer, healthier, happier life. The responsibility for those choices is yours. And so are the rewards.

God wants you to give Him your body. Some people do foolish things with their bodies. God wants your body as a holy sacrifice.

Warren Wiersbe

We shall find in Christ enough of everything we need—for the body, for the mind, and for the spirit—to do what He wants us to do as long as He wants us to do it.

Vance Havner

O, that I could consecrate myself, soul and body, to his service forever; O, that I could give myself up to him, so as never more to attempt to be my own or to have any will or affection improper for those conformed to him.

Lottie Moon

The effective Christians of history have been men and women of great personal discipline—mental discipline, discipline of the body, discipline of the tongue, and discipline of the emotion.

Billy Graham

I'm really busy. Is that a good thing?

THE QUICK ANSWER

Do first things first, and keep your focus on high-priority tasks. And remember this: your highest priority should be your relationship with God and His Son.

Too Busy?

Careful planning puts you ahead in the long run;
hurry and scurry puts you further behind.
Proverbs 21:5 MSG

Everybody knows you're a very busy person. But here's a question: are you able to squeeze time into your hectic schedule for God? Hopefully so! But if you're one of those people who rush through the day with scarcely a single moment to talk with your Creator, it's time to reshuffle your priorities.

You live in a noisy world, a world filled with distractions, frustrations, temptations, and complications. But if you allow the distractions of everyday life to distract you from God's peace, you're doing yourself a big disservice. So here's some good advice: instead of rushing nonstop through the day, slow yourself down long enough to have a few quiet minutes with God.

Nothing is more important than the time you spend with your Heavenly Father. Absolutely nothing. So be still and claim the inner peace that is your spiritual birthright: the peace of Jesus Christ. It is offered freely; it has been paid for in full; it is yours for the asking. So ask. And then share.

Frustration is not the will of God. There is time to do anything and everything that God wants us to do.

Elisabeth Elliot

Noise and words and frenzied, hectic schedules dull our senses, closing our ears to His still, small voice and making us numb to His touch.

Charles Swindoll

In our tense, uptight society where folks are rushing to make appointments they have already missed, a good laugh can be as refreshing as a cup of cold water in the desert.

Barbara Johnson

You're busy with all the pressures of the world around you, but in that busyness you're missing the most important element of all—God's ongoing presence that is available to you.

Bill Hybels

Sometimes my life isn't very exciting. Why should I be excited about life?

THE QUICK ANSWER

Today is a cause for celebration: Psalm 118:24 has clear instructions for the coming day: "This is the day which the LORD has made; let us rejoice and be glad in it." Plan your day—and your life—accordingly.

Celebrate!

At the dedication of the wall of Jerusalem, the Levites were sought out from where they lived and were brought to Jerusalem to celebrate joyfully the dedication with songs of thanksgiving and with the music of cymbals, harps and lyres.

Nehemiah 12:27 NIV

Are you living the triumphant life that God has promised? Or are you, instead, a spiritual shrinking violet? As you ponder that question, consider this: God does not intend that you live a life that is commonplace or mediocre. And He doesn't want you to hide your light "under a basket." Instead, He wants you to "Let your light so shine before men, that they may see your good works and glorify your Father in heaven" (Matthew 5:16

NKJV). In short, God wants you to live a triumphant life so that others might know precisely what it means to be a believer.

The Christian life should be a triumphal celebration, a daily exercise in thanksgiving and praise. Join that celebration today. And while you're at it, make sure that you let everybody—friends, family members, and dates—know that you've joined.

If you can forgive the person you were, accept the person you are, and believe in the person you will become, you are headed for joy. So celebrate your life.

Barbara Johnson

Some of us seem so anxious about avoiding hell that we forget to celebrate our journey toward heaven.

Philip Yancey

The happiest people in the world are not those who have no problems, but the people who have learned to live with those things that are less than perfect.

James Dobson

Christ is the secret, the source, the substance, the center, and the circumference of all true and lasting gladness.

Mrs. Charles E. Cowman

My world is changing faster and faster. What should I do?

THE QUICK ANSWER

If a big change is called for . . . don't be afraid to make a big change—sometimes, one big leap is better than a thousand baby steps.

Always Changing

There is a time for everything,
and a season for every activity under heaven.
Ecclesiastes 3:1 NIV

As you get older, everything around you may seem to be in a state of flux, and you may be required to make lots of adjustments. If all of these events have left your head spinning and your heart pounding, don't worry: although the world is in a state of constant change, God is not.

Even if the changes in your life are unfolding at a furious pace, you can be comforted in the knowledge that your Heavenly Father is the rock that cannot be shaken. His Word promises, "I am the Lord, I do not change" (Malachi 3:6 NKJV).

As graduation gets closer, you're facing an exciting time, a time filled with possibilities and opportunities. But, if your transition to the next phase of life proves to be difficult, don't worry: God is far bigger than any challenge you may face.

Remember that "Jesus Christ is the same yesterday, today, and forever" (Hebrews 13:8 NKJV). And rest assured: It is precisely because your Savior does not change that you can face the transitions of life with courage for today and hope for tomorrow.

Lord, when we are wrong, make us willing to change; and when we are right, make us easy to live with.

Peter Marshall

Sometimes your medicine bottle says, "Shake well before using." That is what God has to do with some of his people. He has to shake them well before they are usable.

Vance Havner

I can't do much about changing the world, but I can do something about bringing God's presence into the world in which He has put me.

Warren Wiersbe

There is not a single thing that Jesus cannot change, control, and conquer because He is the living Lord.

Franklin Graham

You hear lots of people talking about character. But is it really that important?

THE QUICK ANSWER

Remember: Character is more important than popularity.

The Importance of Character

The righteousness of the blameless clears his path,
but the wicked person will fall because of his wickedness.
Proverbs 11:5 HCSB

Character is built slowly over a lifetime. It is the sum of every right decision, every honest word, every noble thought, and every heartfelt prayer. It is forged on the anvil of honorable work and polished by the twin virtues of generosity and humility. Character is a precious thing—difficult to build but easy to tear down. As believers in Christ, we must seek to live each day with discipline, honesty, and faith. When we do, integrity becomes a habit. And God smiles.

Character is both developed and revealed by tests, and all of life is a test.

Rick Warren

Let God use times of waiting to mold and shape your character. Let God use those times to purify your life and make you into a clean vessel for His service.

Henry Blackaby and Claude King

Each one of us is God's special work of art. Through us, He teaches and inspires, delights and encourages, informs and uplifts all those who view our lives. God, the master artist, is most concerned about expressing Himself—His thoughts and His intentions—through what He paints in our characters.

Joni Eareckson Tada

A solid trust is based on a consistent character.

John Maxwell

It is the thoughts and intents of the heart that shape a person's life.

John Eldredge

I make lots of choices every day. How does God want me to choose?

THE QUICK ANSWER

First you'll make choices . . . and before you know it, your choices will make you. So choose carefully.

Your Choices

But Daniel purposed in his heart that he would not defile himself . . . .
Daniel 1:8 KJV

Face facts: your life is a series of choices. From the instant you wake up in the morning until the moment you nod off to sleep at night, you make countless decisions—decisions about the things you do, decisions about the words you speak, and decisions about the way that you choose to direct your thoughts.

As a believer who has been transformed by the radical love of Jesus, you have every reason to make wise choices. But sometimes, when the daily grind threatens to grind you up and spit you out, you may make choices that are displeasing to God. When you do, you'll pay a price because you'll forfeit the happiness and the peace that might otherwise have been yours.

So, as you pause to consider the kind of Christian you are—and the kind of Christian you want to become—ask yourself whether you're sitting on the fence or standing in the light. And while you're at it, ask yourself whether you're choosing friends who help you make smart decisions, not dumb ones. Remember: if you sincerely want to follow in the footsteps of the One from Galilee, you must make choices that are pleasing to Him. He deserves no less . . . and neither, for that matter, do you.

Life is pretty much like a cafeteria line—it offers us many choices, both good and bad. The Christian must have a spiritual radar that detects the difference not only between bad and good but also among good, better, and best.

Dennis Swanberg

We are either the masters or the victims of our attitudes. It is a matter of personal choice. Who we are today is the result of choices we made yesterday. Tomorrow, we will become what we choose today. To change means to choose to change.

John Maxwell

Faith is not a feeling; it is action. It is a willed choice.

Elisabeth Elliot

What should Christ's love mean to me?

THE QUICK ANSWER

Jesus loves me, this I know . . . but how much? Here's how much: Jesus loves you so much that He gave His life so that you might live forever with Him in heaven. And how can you repay Christ's love? By accepting Him into your heart and by obeying His rules. When you do, He will love you and bless you today, tomorrow, and forever.

Christ's Love

I am the good shepherd.
The good shepherd lays down his life for the sheep.
John 10:11 NIV

The Bible makes this promise: Jesus loves you. And how should that make you feel? Well, the fact that Jesus loves you should make you very happy indeed, so happy, in fact, that you try your best to do the things that Jesus wants you to do.

Jesus wants you to welcome Him into your heart, He wants you to love and obey God, and He wants you to be kind to people. These are all very good things to do . . . and the rest is up to you!

Live your lives in love, the same sort of love which Christ gives us, and which He perfectly expressed when He gave Himself as a sacrifice to God.

Corrie ten Boom

It has been the faith of the Son of God who loves me and gave Himself for me that has held me in the darkest valley and the hottest fires and the deepest waters.

Elisabeth Elliot

Jesus is all compassion. He never betrays us.

Catherine Marshall

Christ is like a river that is continually flowing. There are always fresh supplies of water coming from the fountain-head, so that a man may live by it and be supplied with water all his life. So Christ is an ever-flowing fountain; he is continually supplying his people, and the fountain is not spent. They who live upon Christ may have fresh supplies from him for all eternity; they may have an increase of blessedness that is new, and new still, and which never will come to an end.

Jonathan Edwards

It's tempting to skip church. Is it important for me to attend church regularly?

THE QUICK ANSWER

Make it a celebration, not an obligation: What you put into church determines what you get out of it. Your attitude toward worship is   important . . . so celebrate accordingly!

Stay in Church!

Now you are the body of Christ, and individual members of it.
1 Corinthians 12:27 HCSB

The Bible teaches that we should worship God in our hearts and in our churches (Acts 20:28). We have clear instructions to "feed the church of God" and to worship our Creator in the presence of fellow believers.

We live in a world that is teeming with temptations and distractions—a world where good and evil struggle in a constant battle to win our minds, our hearts, and our souls. Our challenge, of course, is to ensure that we cast our lot on the side of God. One way that we remain faithful to Him is through the practice of regular, purposeful worship with our families. When we worship the Father faithfully and fervently, we are blessed.

Our churches are meant to be havens where the caste rules of the world do not apply.

Beth Moore

Be filled with the Holy Spirit; join a church where the members believe the Bible and know the Lord; seek the fellowship of other Christians; learn and be nourished by God's Word and His many promises. Conversion is not the end of your journey—it is only the beginning.

Corrie ten Boom

To model the kingdom of God in the world, the church must not only be a repentant community, committed to truth, but also a holy community.

Chuck Colson

Every time a new person comes to God, every time someone's gifts find expression in the fellowship of believers, every time a family in need is surrounded by the caring church, the truth is affirmed anew: the Church triumphant is alive and well!

Gloria Gaither

Sometimes, I'm tempted to complain. What does the Bible say about complaining?

THE QUICK ANSWER

Perpetual complaining is a bad habit, and it's contagious. Make sure that your friends and family members don't catch it from you!

Don't Complain!

Do everything without complaining or arguing.
Then you will be innocent and without any wrong.
Philippians 2:14-15 NCV

Most of us have more blessings than we can count, yet we can still find reasons to complain about the minor frustrations of everyday life. To do so, of course, is not only shortsighted, but it is also a serious roadblock on the path to spiritual abundance.

Would you like to feel more comfortable about your circumstances and your life? Then promise yourself that you'll do whatever it takes to ensure that you focus your thoughts and energy on the major blessings you've received (not the minor inconveniences you must occasionally endure).

So the next time you're tempted to complain about the inevitable frustrations of everyday living, don't do it! Today and every day, make it a practice to count your blessings, not your hardships. It's the truly decent way to live.

I am sure it is never sadness—a proper, straight, natural response to loss—that does people harm, but all the other things, all the resentment, dismay, doubt, and self-pity with which it is usually complicated.

C. S. Lewis

When you're on the verge of throwing a pity party thanks to your despairing thoughts, go back to the Word of God.

Charles Swindoll

It's your choice: you can either count your blessings or recount your disappointments.

Jim Gallery

He wants us to have a faith that does not complain while waiting, but rejoices because we know our times are in His hands—nail-scarred hands that labor for our highest good.

Kay Arthur

Jesus wept, but he never complained.

C. H. Spurgeon

Sometimes, I feel a lack of confidence. What should I do?

THE QUICK ANSWER

Increase your confidence by living in God's will for your life.

Be Confident

I've told you all this so that trusting me, you will be unshakable and assured, deeply at peace. In this godless world you will continue to experience difficulties.
But take heart! I've conquered the world.
John 16:33 MSG

We Christians have many reasons to be confident. God is in His heaven; Christ has risen, and we are the sheep of His flock. Yet sometimes, even the most devout Christians can become discouraged. Discouragement, however, is not God's way; He is a God of possibility not negativity.

Are you a confident Christian? You should be. God's grace is eternal and His promises are unambiguous. So count your blessings, not your hardships. And live courageously. God is the Giver of all things good, and He watches over you today and forever.

Bible hope is confidence in the future.

Warren Wiersbe

Believe and do what God says. The life-changing consequences will be limitless, and the results will be confidence and peace of mind.

Franklin Graham

If we indulge in any confidence that is not grounded on the Rock of Ages, our confidence is worse than a dream, it will fall on us and cover us with its ruins, causing sorrow and confusion.

C. H. Spurgeon

Jesus gives us the ultimate rest, the confidence we need, to escape the frustration and chaos of the world around us.

Billy Graham

God's omniscience can instill you with a supernatural confidence that can transform your life.

Bill Hybels

What does the Bible say about following my conscience?

THE QUICK ANSWER

Listening to that little voice . . . that quiet little voice inside your head will guide you down the right path if you listen carefully. Very often, your conscience will actually tell you what God wants you to do. So listen, learn, and behave accordingly.

You and Your Conscience

I always do my best to have a clear conscience toward God and men.
Acts 24:16 HCSB

You can keep secrets from other people, but you can't keep secrets from God. God knows what you think and what you do. And, if you want to please God, you must start with good intentions and a pure heart.

If your heart tells you not to do something, don't do it! If your conscience tells you that something is wrong, stop! If you feel ashamed by something you've done, don't do it ever again! Because you can keep secrets from other people some of the time, but God is watching all of the time, and He sees everything, including your heart.

Your conscience is your alarm system. It's your protection.

Charles Stanley

It is neither safe nor prudent to do anything against one's conscience.

Martin Luther

God desires that we become spiritually healthy enough through faith to have a conscience that rightly interprets the work of the Holy Spirit.

Beth Moore

Guilt is a healthy regret for telling God one thing and doing another.

Max Lucado

The voice of the subconscious argues with you, tries to convince you; but the inner voice of God does not argue; it does not try to convince you. It just speaks, and it is self-authenticating.

E. Stanley Jones

At times, I feel discontented with life. How can I find lasting contentment?

THE QUICK ANSWER

Contentment comes, not from your circumstances, but from your attitude.

Finding Real Contentment

The LORD gives strength to his people;
the LORD blesses his people with peace.
Psalm 29:11 NIV

Where can you find contentment? Is it a result of wealth or power or beauty or fame? Hardly. Genuine contentment springs from a peaceful spirit, a clear conscience, and a loving heart (like yours!).

The world seems preoccupied with the search for happiness. We are bombarded with messages telling us that happiness depends upon the way we look or the things we own. These messages are false. Lasting contentment cannot be bought; it must be earned through healthy thoughts, sincere prayers, and good behavior. And if we don't find contentment within ourselves, we will never find it outside ourselves.

So the search for contentment is an internal quest, an exploration of the heart, mind, and soul. You can find contentment—indeed you will find it—if you simply look in the right places. And the best time to start looking in those places is now.

Are you a contented Christian? If so, then you are well aware of the healing power of the risen Christ. But if your spirit is temporarily troubled, perhaps you need to focus less upon your own priorities and more upon God's priorities. When you do, you'll rediscover this life-changing truth: Genuine contentment begins with God . . . and ends there.

Contentment is something we learn by adhering to the basics—cultivating a growing relationship with Jesus Christ, living daily, and knowing that Christ strengthens us for every challenge.

Charles Stanley

The happiness which brings enduring worth to life is not the superficial happiness that is dependent on circumstances. It is the happiness and contentment that fills the soul in the midst of the most distressing of circumstances.

Billy Graham

The circumstances would suggest an utter absence of comfort, yet we find ourselves more than contented.

Lottie Moon

What does the Bible say about conversion?

THE QUICK ANSWER

A true conversion results in a life transformed by Christ and a commitment to following in His footsteps.

You and Your Conversion

Jesus replied, "I assure you: Unless someone is born again,
he cannot see the kingdom of God." "But how can anyone be born
when he is old?" Nicodemus asked Him. "Can he enter his mother's
womb a second time and be born?" Jesus answered,
"I assure you: Unless someone is born of water and the Spirit,
he cannot enter the kingdom of God."
John 3:3–5 HCSB

Think, for a moment, about the "old" you, the person you were before you invited Christ to reign over your heart. Now, think about the "new" you, the person you have become since then. Is there a difference between the "old" you and the "new and improved" version? There should be! And that difference should be noticeable not only to you but also to others.

The Bible clearly teaches that when we welcome Christ into our hearts, we become new creations through Him. Our challenge, of course, is to behave ourselves like new creations. When we do, God fills our hearts, He blesses our endeavors, and transforms our lives . . . forever.

Being a Christian is more than just an instantaneous conversion; it is like a daily process whereby you grow to be more and more like Christ.

Billy Graham

If we accept His invitation to salvation, we live with Him forever. However, if we do not accept because we refuse His only Son as our Savior, then we exclude ourselves from My Father's House. It's our choice.

Anne Graham Lotz

Jesus divided people—everyone—into two classes: the once-born and the twice-born, the unconverted and the converted. No other distinction mattered.

E. Stanley Jones

We cannot change our hearts, but we can change our minds; and when we change our minds, God will change our hearts.

Vance Havner

Sometimes life is tough. When I'm afraid, what should I do?

THE QUICK ANSWER

Courage is trusting God to handle the problems that are simply too big for you to solve.

Finding the Courage Through God

Be strong and courageous, all you who put your hope in the Lord.
Psalm 31:24 HCSB

A storm rose quickly on the Sea of Galilee, and the disciples were afraid. Although they had seen Jesus perform many miracles, the disciples feared for their lives, so they turned to their Savior, and He calmed the waters and the wind.

Sometimes, we, like the disciples, feel threatened by the inevitable storms of life. And when we are fearful, we, too, can turn to Christ for courage and for comfort.

From time to time, all of us, even the most devout believers, experience fear. But, as believers, we can live courageously in the promises of our Lord . . . and we should.

As you take the next step on your life's journey, you can be comforted: Wherever you find yourself, God is there. And, because He cares for you, you can live courageously.

Just as courage is faith in good, so discouragement is faith in evil, and, while courage opens the door to good, discouragement opens it to evil.

Hannah Whitall Smith

Jesus Christ can make the weakest man into a divine dreadnought, fearing nothing.

Oswald Chambers

There comes a time when we simply have to face the challenges in our lives and stop backing down.

John Eldredge

The truth of Christ brings assurance and so removes the former problem of fear and uncertainty.

A. W. Tozer

If a person fears God, he or she has no reason to fear anything else. On the other hand, if a person does not fear God, then fear becomes a way of life.

Beth Moore

NCV: I can find rest in God; only he can save me.

I can't always find time to study my Bible every day. What does the Bible say about my daily devotional?

THE QUICK ANSWER

Get reacquainted with God every day: Would you like a foolproof formula for a better life and better relationships? Here it is: stay in close contact with God.

Every Day with God

Truly my soul silently waits for God; from Him comes my salvation.
Psalm 62:1 NKJV

When it comes to spending time with God, are you a "squeezer" or a "pleaser"? Do you squeeze God into your schedule with a prayer before meals (and maybe, if you've got the time, with a quick visit to church on Sunday)? Or do you please God by talking to Him far more often than that? The answer to this question will determine the direction of your day and the quality of your life.

Each day has 1,440 minutes—do you value your relationship with God enough to spend a few of those minutes with Him? He deserves that much of your time and more—is He receiving it from you? Hopefully so. But if you find that you're simply

God can help you with any of your problems but don't run to him after your problems develop, start now.

"too busy" for a daily chat with your Father in heaven, it's time to take a long, hard look at your priorities and your values.

Warren Wiersbe writes, "Surrender your mind to the Lord at the beginning of each day." And that's sound advice. When you begin each day with your head bowed and your heart lifted, you are reminded of God's love, His protection, and His commandments. Then, you can align your priorities for the coming day with the teachings and commandments that God has placed upon your heart.

So, if you've acquired the unfortunate habit of trying to squeeze God into the corners of your life, it's time to reshuffle the items on your to-do list by placing God first. God wants your undivided attention, not the leftovers of your day. And if you haven't already done so, form the habit of spending quality time with your Father in heaven. He deserves it . . . and so, for that matter, do you.

God is a place of safety you can run to, but it helps if you are running to Him on a daily basis so that you are in familiar territory.

Stormie Omartian

We must appropriate the tender mercy of God every day after conversion or problems quickly develop. We need his grace daily in order to live a righteous life.

Jim Cymbala

What does God's Word say about death?

Death is a fact of life, and nobody knows when or where it's going to happen. So when it comes to making plans for life here on earth and for life eternal, you'd better be ready to live—and to die—right now.

When We Meet Our Maker

And now, brothers and sisters, I want you to know what will happen to the Christians who have died so you will not be full of sorrow like people who have no hope.
1 Thessalonians 4:13 NLT

For Christian believers, death is not an ending; it is a beginning. For Christian believers, the grave is not a final resting-place; it is a place of transition. Yet even when we know our loved ones are at peace with Christ, we still weep bitter tears, not so much for the departed, but instead for ourselves.

God promises that He is "close to the brokenhearted" (Psalm 34:18). In times of intense sadness, we must turn to Him, and we must encourage our friends and family members to do likewise. Death can never claim those who have accepted

Christ as their personal Savior. We have received the gift of life abundant and eternal.

If we really think that home is elsewhere and that this life is a "wandering to find home," why should we not look forward to the arrival?

C. S. Lewis

The believing Christian has hope as he stands at the grave of a loved one who is with the Lord, for he knows that the separation is not forever. It is a glorious truth that those who are in Christ never see each other for the last time.

Billy Graham

Death is swallowed up in victory. Our sorrow is but for a little while, for a better day is coming. We can rejoice when a fellow believer makes his way to his heavenly home.

Dennis Swanberg

We are not meant to die merely in order to be dead. God could not want that for the creatures to whom He has given the breath of life. We die in order to live.

Elisabeth Elliot

Some days are more difficult than others. When times are tough, what should I do?

THE QUICK ANSWER

Difficult days come and go. Stay the course. The sun is shining somewhere and will soon shine on you.

Difficult Days

We also have joy with our troubles, because we know that these troubles produce patience. And patience produces character, and character produces hope.
Romans 5:3-4 NCV

All of us face those occasional days when the traffic jams and the dog gobbles the homework. But, when we find ourselves overtaken by the minor frustrations of life, we must catch ourselves, take a deep breath, and lift our thoughts upward. Although we are here on earth struggling to rise above the distractions of the day, we need never struggle alone. God is here—eternally and faithfully, with infinite patience and love—and, if we reach out to Him, He will restore perspective and peace to our souls.

The strengthening of faith comes from staying with it in the hour of trial. We should not shrink from tests of faith.

Catherine Marshall

When life is difficult, God wants us to have a faith that trusts and waits.

Kay Arthur

If all struggles and sufferings were eliminated, the spirit would no more reach maturity than would the child.

Elisabeth Elliot

The only way to learn a strong faith is to endure great trials. I have learned my faith by standing firm amid the most severe of tests.

George Mueller

Often the trials we mourn are really gateways into the good things we long for.

Hannah Whitall Smith

Some people are hard to get along with. How should I deal with difficult people?

THE QUICK ANSWER

Forgiveness should not be confused with enabling. Even after you've forgiven the difficult person in your life, you are not compelled to accept continued mistreatment from him or her.

Dealing with Difficult People

Hatred stirs up trouble, but love forgives all wrongs.
Proverbs 10:12 NCV

Sometimes, people can be discourteous and cruel. Sometimes people can be unfair, unkind, and unappreciative. Sometimes people get angry and frustrated. So what's a Christian to do? God's answer is straightforward: forgive, forget, and move on. In Luke 6:37, Jesus instructs, "Do not judge, and you will not be judged. Do not condemn, and you will not be condemned. Forgive, and you will be forgiven" (HCSB).

Today and every day, make sure that you're quick to forgive others for their shortcomings. And when other people misbehave (as they most certainly will from time to time), don't pay too much attention. Just forgive those people as quickly as you can, and try to move on . . . as quickly as you can.

A keen sense of humor helps us to overlook the unbecoming, understand the unconventional, tolerate the unpleasant, overcome the unexpected, and outlast the unbearable.

Billy Graham

One way or the other, God, who thought up the family in the first place, has the very best idea of how to bring sense to the chaos of broken relationships we see all around us. I really believe that if I remain still and listen a lot, He will share some solutions with me so I can share them with others.

Jill Briscoe

Some folks cause happiness wherever they go, others whenever they go.

Barbara Johnson

Sour godliness is the devil's religion.

John Wesley

You can be sure you are abiding in Christ if you are able to have a Christlike love toward the people that irritate you the most.

Vonette Bright

When I'm disappointed with the way things have turned out, what should I do?

THE QUICK ANSWER

Don't spend too much time asking "Why me, Lord?" Instead, ask, "What now, Lord?" and then get to work. When you do, you'll feel much better.

Dealing with Disappointments

When you go through deep waters and great trouble,
I will be with you. When you go through the rivers of difficulty,
you will not drown! When you walk through the fire of oppression,
you will not be burned up; the flames will not consume you.
For I am the Lord, your God . . . .
Isaiah 43:2-3 NLT

Face facts: some days are more wonderful than other days. Sometimes, everything seems to go right, and on other days, many things seem to go wrong. But here's something to remember: even when you're disappointed with the way things turn out, God is near . . . and He loves you very much!

If you're disappointed, worried, sad, or afraid, you can talk to your parents and to God. And you will certainly feel better when you do!

Each of us has something broken in our lives: a broken promise, a broken dream, a broken marriage, a broken heart . . . and we must decide how we're going to deal with our brokenness. We can wallow in self-pity or regret, accomplishing nothing and having no fun or joy in our circumstances; or we can determine with our will to take a few risks, get out of our comfort zone, and see what God will do to bring unexpected delight in our time of need.

Luci Swindoll

Though our pain and our disappointment and the details of our suffering may differ, there is an abundance of God's grace and peace available to each of us.

Charles Swindoll

Why should I ever resist any delay or disappointment, any affliction or oppression or humiliation, when I know God will use it in my life to make me like Jesus and to prepare me for heaven?

Kay Arthur

What does the Bible say about discipleship?

THE QUICK ANSWER

Talk is cheap. Real ministry has legs. When it comes to being a disciple, make sure that you back up your words with deeds.

The Decision to Be His Disciple

You did not choose Me, but I chose you.
I appointed you that you should go out and produce fruit,
and that your fruit should remain, so that whatever you ask
the Father in My name, He will give you.
John 15:16 HCSB

Jesus' group of twelve disciples came from all walks of life: blue collar and professionals, including fishermen and a tax collector. They were from different political spectrums, including some passionate zealots. These twelve men came with diverse personalities and emotional traits: from Peter the impulsive to Thomas the doubter.

God is still in the business of acquiring disciples: ditch diggers and presidents; Republicans, Democrats, and independents; introverts and extroverts. His only criterion is that you believe in Him and be willing to sacrifice your all for His kingdom's work.

Real men and women become disciples by forsaking all and giving their lives to Christ. It is not easy, but those who stay the course are rewarded with a life of passion and purpose.

It is the secret of true discipleship to bear the cross, to acknowledge the death sentence that has been passed on self, and to deny any right that self has to rule over us.

Andrew Murray

How often it occurs to me, as it must to you, that is far easier simply to cooperate with God!

Beth Moore

A follower is never greater than his leader; a follower never draws attention to himself.

Franklin Graham

As we seek to become disciples of Jesus Christ, we should never forget that the word disciple is directly related to the word discipline. To be a disciple of the Lord Jesus Christ is to know his discipline.

Dennis Swanberg

QUESTION 30

What does the Bible say about discipline?

THE QUICK ANSWER

A disciplined lifestyle gives you more control: The more disciplined you become, the more you can take control over your life (which, by the way, is far better than letting your life take control over you).

Discipline Now

*No discipline seems enjoyable at the time, but painful.
Later on, however, it yields the fruit of peace
and righteousness to those who have been trained by it.*
Hebrews 12:11 HCSB

Students everywhere understand the profound sense of joy that accompanies two little words: "School's out!" In a brief, two-word exclamatory sentence, so much is said. "School's out!" means no more homework, no more papers, no more grades, and no more standardized tests. "School's out!" means it's time for a much-needed break from the daily grind. "School's out!" means it's time to put the books—and the worries—away. But before the celebration gets out of hand, be forewarned: "School's out!" does not mean that our work is done. To the contrary, the real work is probably just beginning.

100 QUESTIONS TEENS ASK

Those who study the Bible are confronted again and again with God's intention that His children lead disciplined lives. God doesn't reward laziness. To the contrary, He expects believers to adopt a disciplined approach to their lives. In Proverbs 28:19, the message is clear: work diligently and consistently, and then expect a bountiful harvest. But never expect the harvest to precede the labor.

When you graduate, you will have earned the right to proclaim "School's out!" at the top of your lungs. And when all the shouting is over, remember that God rewards discipline just as certainly as He punishes indolence. And if you're not sure what the word *indolence* means, then school isn't really out yet, now is it? Your dictionary is in that stack of books over there in the corner. Happy reading!

The Bible calls for discipline and a recognition of authority. Children must learn this at home.

Billy Graham

Discipline is training that develops and corrects.

Charles Stanley

Work is doing it. Discipline is doing it every day. Diligence is doing it well every day.

Dave Ramsey

QUESTION 31

Sometimes I have doubts about my future and doubts about my faith. What should I do?

THE QUICK ANSWER

When you have doubts, it is important to take those doubts to the Lord.

When You Have Doubts

Purify your hearts, ye double-minded.
James 4:8 KJV

Have you ever wondered if God hears your prayers? If so, you're not the first person to have questions like that. Doubts come in several shapes and sizes: doubts about God, doubts about the future, and doubts about your own abilities, for starters. And what, precisely, does God's Word say in response to these doubts? The Bible is clear: when you are beset by doubts, of whatever kind, you must draw yourself nearer to God through worship and through prayer. When you do, God, the loving Father who has never left your side, draws ever closer to you (James 4:8).

Is prayer an integral part of your daily life, or is it a hit-or-miss habit? Do you "pray without ceasing," or is prayer an afterthought? If your prayer life leaves something to be desired, you're robbing yourself of a deeper relationship with God. And how can you rectify that situation? By praying more frequently and more fervently.

The quality of your spiritual life will be in direct proportion to the quality of your prayer life: the more you pray, the closer you will feel to God. So today, instead of turning things over in your mind, turn them over to God in prayer. Instead of worrying about your next decision, ask God to lead the way. Don't limit your prayers to the dinner table or the bedside table. Pray constantly about things great and small. When you do, your Heavenly Father will take care of you . . . and your doubts will take care of themselves.

Doubting may temporarily disturb, but will not permanently destroy, your faith in Christ.

Charles Swindoll

A life lived in God is not lived on the plane of feelings, but of the will.

Elisabeth Elliot

Seldom do you enjoy the luxury of making decisions that are based on enough evidence to absolutely silence all skepticism.

Bill Hybels

I have big dreams. What should I do about them?

THE QUICK ANSWER

Making your dreams come true requires work. John Maxwell writes, "The gap between your vision and your present reality can only be filled through a commitment to maximize your potential." Enough said.

Big Dreams

I came so they can have real and eternal life,
more and better life than they ever dreamed of.
John 10:10 MSG

How big are you willing to dream? Are you willing to entertain the possibility that God has big plans in store for you? Or are you convinced that your future is so dim that you'd better wear night goggles? Well here's the facts: if you're a believer in the One from Galilee, you have an incredibly bright future ahead of you . . . here on earth and in heaven. That's why you have every right to dream big.

Concentration camp survivor Corrie ten Boom observed, "Every experience God gives us, every person he brings into our lives, is the perfect preparation for the future that only he can see." These words apply to you.

100 QUESTIONS TEENS ASK

Are you excited about the opportunities of today and thrilled by the possibilities of tomorrow? Do you confidently expect God to lead you to a place of abundance, peace, and joy? And, when your days on earth are over, do you expect to receive the priceless gift of eternal life? If you trust God's promises, and if you have welcomed God's Son into your heart, then you believe that your future is intensely and eternally bright.

It takes courage to dream big dreams. You will discover that courage when you do three things: accept the past, trust God to handle the future, and make the most of the time He has given you today.

Nothing is too difficult for God, and no dreams are too big for Him—not even yours. So start living—and dreaming—accordingly.

Do not limit the limitless God! With Him, face the future unafraid because you are never alone.

Mrs. Charles E. Cowman

Allow your dreams a place in your prayers and plans. God-given dreams can help you move into the future He is preparing for you.

Barbara Johnson

To make your dream come true, you have to stay awake.

Dennis Swanberg

I have lots of responsibilities. What should I do about them?

THE QUICK ANSWER

When you accept your duties and fulfill them, you'll feel good about yourself. When you avoid your obligations, you won't. Act accordingly.

Be Responsible!

But each person should examine his own work,
and then he will have a reason for boasting in himself alone,
and not in respect to someone else.
For each person will have to carry his own load.
Galatians 6:4-5 HCSB

Nobody needs to tell you the obvious: You have lots of responsibilities—obligations to yourself, to your family, to your community, and to your God. And which of these duties should take priority? The answer can be found in Matthew 6:33: "But seek first the kingdom of God and His righteousness, and all these things will be provided for you" (HCSB).

When you "seek first the kingdom of God," all your other obligations have a way of falling into place. When you obey

God's Word and seek His will, your many responsibilities don't seem quite so burdensome. When you honor God with your time, your talents, and your prayers, you'll be much more likely to count your blessings instead of your troubles.

So do yourself and your loved ones a favor: take all your duties seriously, especially your duties to God. When you do, you'll discover that pleasing your Father in heaven isn't just the right thing to do; it's also the best way to live.

When the law of God is written on our hearts, our duty will be our delight.

Matthew Henry

There is an active practice of holiness as we carry out, for the glory of God, the ordinary duties of each day, faithfully fulfilling the responsibilities given us. The passive practice consists in loving acceptance of the unexpected, be it welcome or unwelcome, remembering that we have a wise and sovereign Lord who works in mysterious ways and is never taken by surprise.

Elisabeth Elliot

If you seek to know the path of your duty, use God as your compass.

C. H. Spurgeon

Sometimes, my emotions get the better of me. What should I do?

THE QUICK ANSWER

When others lose control of their emotions, try not to become caught up in the frenzy.

Controlling Your Emotions

All bitterness, anger and wrath, insult and slander must be removed from you, along with all wickedness. And be kind and compassionate to one another, forgiving one another, just as God also forgave you in Christ.
Ephesians 4:31-32 HCSB

Who is in charge of your emotions? Is it you, or have you formed the unfortunate habit of letting other people—or troubling situations—determine the quality of your thoughts and the direction of your day? If you're wise—and if you'd like to build a better life for yourself and your loved ones—you'll learn to control your emotions before your emotions control you.

Human emotions can be highly variable, decidedly unpredictable, and often unreliable. Our emotions are like the weather, only far more fickle. So we must learn to live by faith, not by the ups and downs of our own emotional roller coasters.

Sometime during this day, you will probably be gripped by a strong negative feeling. Distrust it. Reign it in. Test it. And turn it over to God. Your emotions will inevitably change; God will not. So trust Him completely as you watch those negative feelings slowly evaporate into thin air—which, of course, they will.

Emotions we have not poured out in the safe hands of God can turn into feelings of hopelessness and depression. God is safe.

Beth Moore

The only serious mistake we can make is the mistake that Psalm 121 prevents: the mistake of supposing that God's interest in us waxes and wanes in response to our spiritual temperature.

Eugene Peterson

Don't bother much about your feelings. When they are humble, loving, brave, give thanks for them; when they are conceited, selfish, cowardly, ask to have them altered. In neither case are they you, but only a thing that happens to you. What matters is your intentions and your behavior.

C. S. Lewis

What does the Bible say about empathy?

THE QUICK ANSWER

Empathy is just another word for love.

Thinking About the Other Person

Be hospitable to one another without complaining.
1 Peter 4:9 HCSB

We live in a world that is, on occasion, a frightening place. Sometimes, we sustain life-altering losses that are so profound and so tragic that it seems we could never recover. But, with God's help and with the help of encouraging family members and friends, we can recover.

In times of need, God's Word is clear: we must offer comfort to those in need by sharing not only our courage but also our faith.

Do you know someone who needs a helping hand or an encouraging word? Of course you do. And the very best day to extend your helping hand is this one. So as you make your plans for the day ahead, look for somebody to help. When you do, you'll be a powerful example to your family and a worthy servant to your Creator.

Deep in the dark night of the suffering soul comes a moment when nothing intellectual or psychological matters. It is the time of the touch, the tender touch, a hand held, a cheek kissed, a holy embrace that conveys more to the human spirit than anything from tongue or pen.

Bill Bright

Before you can dry another's tears, you too must weep.

Barbara Johnson

Empathy is just another word for love.

Jim Gallery

Those who mourn are those who have allowed themselves to feel real feelings because they care about other people.

Barbara Johnson

QUESTION 36

So many people around me seem to need encouragement. What should I do?

THE QUICK ANSWER

Do you want to be successful and go far in life? Encourage others to do the same. You can't lift other people up without lifting yourself up, too. And remember the words of Oswald Chambers: "God grant that we may not hinder those who are battling their way slowly into the light."

The Gift of Encouragement

Therefore encourage one another and build each other up as you are already doing.
1 Thessalonians 5:11 HCSB

The words that we speak have the power to do great good or great harm. If we speak words of encouragement and hope, we can lift others up. And that's exactly what God commands us to do!

Sometimes, when we feel uplifted and secure, it's easy to speak kind words. Other times, when we are discouraged or tired, we can scarcely summon the energy to uplift ourselves, much less anyone else. God intends that we speak words of kindness, wisdom, and truth, no matter our circumstances, no matter our emotions. When we do, we share a priceless gift with the world, and we give glory to the One who gave His life for us. As believers, we must do no less.

———————————————

God is still in the process of dispensing gifts, and He uses ordinary individuals like us to develop those gifts in other people.

Howard Hendricks

He climbs highest who helps another up.

Zig Ziglar

No journey is complete that does not lead through some dark valleys. We can properly comfort others only with the comfort we ourselves have been given by God.

Vance Havner

One of the ways God refills us after failure is through the blessing of Christian fellowship. Just experiencing the joy of simple activities shared with other children of God can have a healing effect on us.

Anne Graham Lotz

What does the Bible say about enthusiasm?

THE QUICK ANSWER

Be enthusiastic about your faith: John Wesley wrote, "You don't have to advertise a fire. Get on fire for God and the world will come to watch you burn." When you allow yourself to become extremely enthusiastic about your faith, other people will notice—and so will God.

Enthused About Life

Whatever work you do, do your best, because you are going to the grave, where there is no working . . . .
Ecclesiastes 9:10 NCV

Genuine, heartfelt Christianity is contagious. If you enjoy a life-altering relationship with God, that relationship will have an impact on others—perhaps a profound impact.

Are you genuinely excited about your faith? And do you make your enthusiasm known to those around you? Or are you a "silent ambassador" for Christ? God's preference is clear: He intends that you stand before others and proclaim your faith.

Does Christ reign over your life? Then share your testimony and your excitement. The world needs both.

100 QUESTIONS TEENS ASK

We act as though comfort and luxury were the chief requirements of life, when all we need to make us really happy is something to be enthusiastic about.

Charles Kingsley

When we wholeheartedly commit ourselves to God, there is nothing mediocre or run-of-the-mill about us. To live for Christ is to be passionate about our Lord and about our lives.

Jim Gallery

Wherever you are, be all there. Live to the hilt every situation you believe to be the will of God.

Jim Elliot

Don't take hold of a thing unless you want that thing to take hold of you.

E. Stanley Jones

It is a remarkable thing that some of the most optimistic and enthusiastic people you will meet are those who have been through intense suffering.

Warren Wiersbe

Sometimes, I'm envious of other people. What should I do?

THE QUICK ANSWER

You can be envious, or you can be happy, but you can't be both. Envy and happiness can't live at the same time in the same brain.

Envy Is Poison

Do not covet your neighbor's house . . .
or anything that belongs to your neighbor.
Exodus 20:17 HCSB

Because we are frail, imperfect human beings, we are sometimes envious of others. But God's Word warns us that envy is wrong. So if we are wise, we will guard ourselves against the natural tendency to feel resentment and jealousy when other people experience good fortune.

Have you ever felt the pangs of envy when a friend or family member experienced good luck? Of have you been resentful when others received recognition or earned advancement? If so, here's a simple suggestion that is guaranteed to improve your attitude and lift your spirits: fill your heart with God's love, God's promises, and God's Son . . . and when you do, you'll discover that there's no room left for envy, resentment, or regret.

Discontent dries up the soul.

Elisabeth Elliot

Contentment comes when we develop an attitude of gratitude for the important things we do have in our lives that we tend to take for granted if we have our eyes staring longingly at our neighbor's stuff.

Dave Ramsey

Too many Christians envy the sinners their pleasure and the saints their joy because they don't have either one.

Martin Luther

What God asks, does, or requires of others is not my business; it is His.

Kay Arthur

When you worry about what you don't have, you won't be able to enjoy what you do have.

Charles Swindoll

QUESTION 39

This world can be a crazy place. What should I do about the evils that I encounter?

THE QUICK ANSWER

There is darkness in this world, but God's light can overpower any darkness.

Evil Is All Around Us

You were taught to leave your old self—to stop living the evil way you lived before. That old self becomes worse, because people are fooled by the evil things they want to do. But you were taught to be made new in your hearts, to become a new person. That new person is made to be like God—made to be truly good and holy.
Ephesians 4:22–24 NCV

Face facts: this world is inhabited by quite a few people who are very determined to do evil things. The devil and his human helpers are working 24/7 to cause pain and heartbreak in every corner of the globe . . . including your corner. So you'd better beware.

Your job, if you choose to accept it, is to recognize evil and fight it. The moment that you decide to fight evil whenever you see it, you can no longer be a lukewarm, halfhearted Christian.

And, when you are no longer a lukewarm Christian, God rejoices while the devil despairs.

When will you choose to get serious about fighting the evils of our world? Before you answer that question, consider this: in the battle of good versus evil, the devil never takes a day off . . . and neither should you.

Christianity isn't a religion about going to Sunday school, potluck suppers, being nice, holding car washes, sending your secondhand clothes off to Mexico—as good as those things might be. This is a world at war.

John Eldredge

We are in a continual battle with the spiritual forces of evil, but we will triumph when we yield to God's leading and call on His powerful presence in prayer.

Shirley Dobson

Where God's ministers are most successful, there the powers of darkness marshal their forces for the conflict.

Lottie Moon

Holiness has never been the driving force of the majority. It is, however, mandatory for anyone who wants to enter the kingdom.

Elisabeth Elliot

What does the Bible say about the example that I should set for others?

THE QUICK ANSWER

Your life is a sermon. What kind of sermon will you preach? The words you choose to speak may have some impact on others, but not nearly as much impact as the life you choose to live.

What Kind of Example?

Do everything without grumbling and arguing,
so that you may be blameless and pure.
Philippians 2:14–15 HCSB

How do people know that you're a Christian? Well, you can tell them, of course. And make no mistake about it: talking about your faith in God is a very good thing to do. But simply telling people about Jesus isn't enough. You must also be willing to show people how an extremely devoted Christian (like you) should behave.

Is your life a picture book of your creed? Do your actions line up with your beliefs? Are you willing to practice the philosophy that you preach? If so, congratulations. If not, it's time for a change.

Like it or not, your behavior is a powerful example to others. The question is not whether you will be an example to your family and friends; the question is what kind of example will you be.

Corrie ten Boom advised, "Don't worry about what you do not understand. Worry about what you do understand in the Bible but do not live by." And that's sound advice because your family and friends are always watching . . . and so, for that matter, is God.

Living life with a consistent spiritual walk deeply influences those we love most.

Vonette Bright

We urgently need people who encourage and inspire us to move toward God and away from the world's enticing pleasures.

Jim Cymbala

In our faith we follow in someone's steps. In our faith we leave footprints to guide others. It's the principle of discipleship.

Max Lucado

Your light is the truth of the Gospel message itself as well as your witness as to Who Jesus is and what He has done for you. Don't hide it.

Anne Graham Lotz

Sometimes, despite my best efforts, I am unsuccessful. What does the Bible say about failure?

THE QUICK ANSWER

Failure is never permanent . . . unless you give up and quit trying.

Beyond Failure

If you listen to constructive criticism,
you will be at home among the wise.
Proverbs 15:31 NLT

The occasional disappointments and failures of life are inevitable. Such setbacks are simply the price that we must occasionally pay for our willingness to take risks as we follow our dreams. But even when we encounter bitter disappointments, we must never lose faith.

The reassuring words of Hebrews 10:36 remind us that when we persevere, we will eventually receive that which God has promised. What's required is perseverance, not perfection.

When we encounter the inevitable difficulties of life here on earth, God stands ready to protect us. Our responsibility, of course, is to ask Him for protection. When we call upon Him in heartfelt prayer, He will answer—in His own time and according to His own plan—and He will heal us. And, while we are waiting for God's plans to unfold and for His healing touch to restore us, we can be comforted in the knowledge that our Creator can overcome any obstacle, even if we cannot.

Failure is one of life's most powerful teachers. How we handle our failures determines whether we're going to simply "get by" in life or "press on."

Beth Moore

God is able to take mistakes, when they are committed to Him, and make of them something for our good and for His glory.

Ruth Bell Graham

If you learn from a defeat, you have not really lost.

Zig Ziglar

The enemy of our souls loves to taunt us with past failures, wrongs, disappointments, disasters, and calamities. And if we let him continue doing this, our life becomes a long and dark tunnel, with very little light at the end.

Charles Swindoll

QUESTION 42

What does the Bible say about the power of faith?

THE QUICK ANSWER

Faith in God is contagious . . . and when it comes to your family's spiritual journey, no one's faith is more contagious than yours! Act, pray, praise, and trust God with the certain knowledge that your friends and family are watching . . . carefully!

The Power of Faith

Be alert, stand firm in the faith, be brave and strong.
1 Corinthians 16:13 HCSB

In the months and years ahead, your faith will be tested many times. Every life—including yours—is a series of successes and failures, celebrations and disappointments, joys and sorrows. Every step of the way, through every triumph and tragedy, God will stand by your side and strengthen you . . . if you have faith in Him. Jesus taught His disciples that if they had faith, they could move mountains. You can too.

If you place your faith, your trust, indeed your life in the hands of Christ Jesus, you'll be amazed at the marvelous things He can do with you and through you. Faith is a willingness to believe in things that are unseeable and to trust in things that are unknowable.

Today and every day, strengthen your faith through praise, through worship, through Bible study, and through prayer. God has big plans for you, so trust His plans and strengthen your faith in Him. With God, all things are possible, and He stands ready to help you accomplish miraculous things with your life . . . if you have faith.

A faith that hasn't been tested can't be trusted.

Adrian Rogers

Just as our faith strengthens our prayer life, so do our prayers deepen our faith. Let us pray often, starting today, for a deeper, more powerful faith.

Shirley Dobson

There are a lot of things in life that are difficult to understand. Faith allows the soul to go beyond what the eyes can see.

John Maxwell

The popular idea of faith is of a certain obstinate optimism: the hope, tenaciously held in the face of trouble, that the universe is fundamentally friendly and things may get better.

J. I. Packer

What does the Bible say about family life?

THE QUICK ANSWER

Let your family members know that you love them by the things you say and the things you do. And, never take your family for granted; they deserve your very best treatment!

You and Your Family

Choose for yourselves today the one you will worship . . . .
As for me and my family, we will worship the Lord.
Joshua 24:15 HCSB

Do you sometimes take your family for granted? If so, welcome to the club. At times, it's surprisingly easy to ignore the people we love the most. After all, we know that they'll still love us no matter what we do. But whenever we ignore our loved ones, we're doing a big disservice to our loved ones and to ourselves.

A loving family is a treasure from God. If God has blessed you with a close knit, supportive clan, offer a word of thanks to your Creator because He has given you one of His most precious earthly possessions. Your obligation, in response to God's gift, is to treat your family in ways that are consistent with His commandments.

You live in a fast-paced, demanding world, a place where life can be difficult and pressures can be intense. As those pressures build, you may tend to focus so intently upon your obligations that you lose sight, albeit temporarily, of your spiritual and emotional needs (that's one reason why a regular daily devotional time is so important; it offers a badly-needed dose of perspective).

So the next time your family life becomes a little stressful, remember this: That little band of men, women, kids, and babies is a priceless treasure on temporary loan from the Father above. And it's your responsibility to praise God for that gift—and to act accordingly.

———————————————

Living life with a consistent spiritual walk deeply influences those we love most.

Vonette Bright

A man ought to live so that everybody knows he is a Christian, and most of all, his family ought to know.

D. L. Moody

The only true source of meaning in life is found in love for God and his son Jesus Christ, and love for mankind, beginning with our own families.

James Dobson

QUESTION 44

What does the Bible say about the way that I should handle money?

THE QUICK ANSWER

Don't fall in love with "stuff." We live in a society that worships "stuff"—don't fall into that trap. Remember this: "stuff" is highly overrated. Worship God almighty, not the almighty dollar (Proverbs 11:28).

You and Your Money

Honor the Lord with your wealth and the firstfruits from all your crops. Then your barns will be full, and your wine barrels will overflow with new wine.
Proverbs 3:9-10 NCV

God's Word is not only a roadmap to eternal life; it is also an indispensable guidebook for life here on earth. As such, the Bible has much to say about your life and your finances.

God's Word can be a roadmap to a place of righteousness and abundance. Make it your roadmap. God's wisdom can be a light to guide your steps. Claim it as your light. God's Word can be an invaluable tool for crafting a better day and a better life. Make it your tool. And finally, God's Word can help you organize your financial life in such a way that you have less need to worry and more time to celebrate His glorious creation. If that sounds appealing, open your Bible, read its instructions, and follow them.

Here's a recipe for handling money wisely: Take a heaping helping of common sense, add a sizeable portion of self-discipline, and mix with prayer.

Marie T. Freeman

I sincerely believe that once Christians have been educated in God's plan for their finances, they will find a freedom they had never known before.

Larry Burkett

If you work hard and maintain an attitude of gratitude, you'll find it easier to manage your finances every day.

John Maxwell

Discipline understands that the best way to get rich quick is to get rich slow.

Dave Ramsey

QUESTION 45

What does the Bible say about following in Jesus' footsteps?

THE QUICK ANSWER

If you want to follow in Christ's footsteps . . . welcome Him into your heart, obey His commandments, and share His never-ending love.

Following Christ

We encouraged, comforted, and implored each one of you to walk worthy of God, who calls you into His own kingdom and glory.
1 Thessalonians 2:12 HCSB

Jesus loved you so much that He endured unspeakable humiliation and suffering for you. How will you respond to Christ's sacrifice? Will you take up His cross and follow Him, (Luke 9:23) or will you choose another path? When you place your hopes squarely at the foot of the cross, when you place Jesus squarely at the center of your life, you will be blessed.

The 19th-century writer Hannah Whitall Smith observed, "The crucial question for each of us is this: What do you think of Jesus, and do you yet have a personal acquaintance with Him?" Indeed, the answer to that question determines the quality, the course, and the direction of our lives today and for all eternity.

The old familiar hymn begins, "What a friend we have in Jesus . . . ." No truer words were ever penned. Jesus is the sovereign Friend and ultimate Savior of mankind. Christ showed enduring love for His believers by willingly sacrificing His own life so that we might have eternal life. Now, it is our turn to become His friend.

When you graduate, it will be time to take the next step on your life's journey; make certain that you take that step with Christ by your side. Accept His love, obey His teachings, and share His message with your neighbors and with the world. When you do, you will demonstrate that your acquaintance with the Master is not a passing fancy; it is, instead, the cornerstone and the touchstone of your life.

Living life with a consistent spiritual walk deeply influences those we love most.

Vonette Bright

The cross that Jesus commands you and me to carry is the cross of submissive obedience to the will of God, even when His will includes suffering and hardship and things we don't want to do.

Anne Graham Lotz

Sometimes it's hard for me to forgive the people who have hurt me. What does the Bible say about forgiveness?

THE QUICK ANSWER

Forgive . . . and keep forgiving! Sometimes, you may forgive someone once and then, at a later time, become angry at the very same person again. If so, you must forgive that person again and again . . . until it sticks!

Forgiveness Now

If you forgive those who sin against you,
your Heavenly Father will forgive you. But if you refuse to forgive
others, your Father will not forgive your sins.
Matthew 6:14-15 NLT

Whenever people hurt us—whether emotionally, physically, financially, or otherwise—it's hard to forgive. But God's Word is clear: we must forgive other people, even when we'd rather not. So, if you're angry with anybody (or if you're upset by something you yourself have done), it's now time to forgive.

God instructs you to treat other people exactly as you wish to be treated. And since you want to be forgiven for the mistakes that you make, you must be willing to extend forgiveness to other people for the mistakes that they have made.

If you can't seem to forgive someone, you should keep asking God for help until you do. And of this you can be sure: if you keep asking for God's help, He will give it.

Forgiveness is actually the best revenge because it not only sets us free from the person we forgive, but it frees us to move into all that God has in store for us.

Stormie Omartian

We are products of our past, but we don't have to be prisoners of it. God specializes in giving people a fresh start.

Rick Warren

Miracles broke the physical laws of the universe; forgiveness broke the moral rules.

Philip Yancey

Bitterness is the trap that snares the hunter.

Max Lucado

Forgiveness is contagious. First you forgive them, and pretty soon, they'll forgive you, too.

Marie T. Freeman

QUESTION 47

What does the Bible say about my friends?

THE QUICK ANSWER

Remember the first rule of friendship: it's the Golden one, and it starts like this: "Do unto others . . ." (Matthew 7:12).

You and Your Friends

Greater love has no one than this,
that he lay down his life for his friends.
John 15:13 NIV

Our world is filled with pressures: some good, some bad. The pressures that we feel to follow God's rules are the good kind of pressures (and the friends who make us want to obey God are good friends). But sometimes, we may feel pressure to misbehave, pressure from friends who want us to disobey the rules.

If you want to please God and your parents, make friends with people who behave themselves. When you do, you'll be much more likely to behave yourself, too . . . and that's a very good thing.

Though I know intellectually how vulnerable I am to pride and power, I am the last one to know when I succumb to their seduction. That's why spiritual Lone Rangers are so dangerous—and why we must depend on trusted brothers and sisters who love us enough to tell us the truth.

Chuck Colson

Don't bypass the potential for meaningful friendships just because of differences. Explore them. Embrace them. Love them.

Luci Swindoll

Friendships are living organisms at work. They continue to unfold, change, and emerge.

Barbara Johnson

The glory of friendship is not the outstretched hand or the kindly smile or the joy of companionship. It is the spiritual inspiration that comes to one when he discovers that someone else believes in him and is willing to trust him with his friendship.

Corrie ten Boom

In friendship, God opens your eyes to the glories of Himself.

Joni Eareckson Tada

Sometimes I'm worried about the future. What does God's Word say about my future?

THE QUICK ANSWER

Focus more on future opportunities than on past disappointments.

Your Very Bright Future

"I say this because I know what I am planning for you,"
says the Lord. "I have good plans for you, not plans to hurt you.
I will give you hope and a good future."
Jeremiah 29:11 NCV

How can you make smart choices if you're unwilling to trust God and obey Him? The answer, of course, is that you can't. That's why you should trust God in everything (and that means entrusting your future to God).

How bright is your future? Well, if you're a faithful believer, God's plans for you are so bright that you'd better wear shades. But here are some important follow-up questions: How bright do you believe your future to be? Are you expecting a terrific tomorrow, or are you dreading a terrible one? The answer you give will have a powerful impact on the way tomorrow turns out.

Do you trust in the ultimate goodness of God's plan for your life? Will you face tomorrow's challenges with optimism and hope? You should. After all, God created you for a very important reason: His reason. And you have important work to do: His work.

Today, as you live in the present and look to the future, remember that God has an amazing plan for you. Act—and believe—accordingly.

Do not limit the limitless God! With Him, face the future unafraid because you are never alone.

Mrs. Charles E. Cowman

You can look forward with hope, because one day there will be no more separation, no more scars, and no more suffering in My Father's House. It's the home of your dreams!

Anne Graham Lotz

The future lies all before us. Shall it only be a slight advance upon what we usually do? Ought it not to be a bound, a leap forward to altitudes of endeavor and success undreamed of before?

Annie Armstrong

Every saint has a past—every sinner has a future!

Anonymous

What does the Bible have to say about generosity?

THE QUICK ANSWER

Would you like to be a little happier? Try sharing a few more of the blessings that God has bestowed upon you. In other words, if you want to be happy, be generous. And if you want to be unhappy, be greedy.

The Wisdom to Be Generous

Above all, love each other deeply,
because love covers a multitude of sins.
1 Peter 4:8 NIV

The Bible makes an important promise: If you give, you will receive. If you give generously of your time, your possessions, your talents, and your love, you will be blessed by the Creator.

Your life is a tapestry of choices. Every day you face inevitable choices concerning the things you should keep for yourself and the things you should give away. When in doubt, try to be a little more generous than necessary.

Be quick to share a smile, an encouraging word, a pat on the back, a helping hand, or a heartfelt hug. Be more concerned with giving than getting. Weave the habit of generosity into the fabric of your day. When you do, everybody wins, and you're the biggest winner of all.

God does not supply money to satisfy our every whim and desire. His promise is to meet our needs and provide an abundance so that we can help other people.

Larry Burkett

Charity—giving to the poor—is an essential part of Christian morality. . . . I do not believe one can settle how much we ought to give. I am afraid the only safe rule is to give more than we can spare.

C. S. Lewis

I can usually sense that a leading is from the Holy Spirit when it calls me to humble myself, to serve somebody, to encourage somebody, or to give something away. Very rarely will the evil one lead us to do those kind of things.

Bill Hybels

Jesus had a loving heart. If he dwells within us, hatred and bitterness will never rule us.

Billy Graham

I want to sense a calling from God. What does the Bible say about that?

THE QUICK ANSWER

God calls you to a life that is perfectly suited for you, a life that will bring happiness and satisfaction to yourself and to others.

God's Calling

I, therefore, the prisoner in the Lord,
urge you to walk worthy of the calling you have received.
Ephesians 4:1 HCSB

Call is calling you to follow a specific path that He has chosen for your life. And it is vitally important that you heed that call. Otherwise, your talents and opportunities may go unused.

Have you already heard God's call? And are you pursuing it with vigor? If so, you're both fortunate and wise. But if you have not yet discovered what God intends for you to do with your life, keep searching and keep praying until you discover why the Creator put you here.

Remember: God has important work for you to do—work that no one else on earth can accomplish but you. The Creator has placed you in a particular location, amid particular people, with unique opportunities to serve. And He has given you all the tools you need to succeed. So listen for His voice, watch for His signs, and prepare yourself for the call that is sure to come.

––––––––––––––––––––––

When you become consumed by God's call on your life, everything will take on new meaning and significance. You will begin to see every facet of your life, including your pain, as a means through which God can work to bring others to Himself.

Charles Stanley

If God has called you, do not spend time looking over your shoulder to see who is following you.

Corrie ten Boom

God tends to lead us through gentle spiritual promptings.

Bill Hybels

God's help is near and always available, but it is only given to those who seek it.

Max Lucado

God never calls without enabling us. In other words, if he calls you to do something, he makes it possible for you to do it.

Luci Swindoll

If I want God to guide me, what should I do?

THE QUICK ANSWER

Pray for guidance. When you seek it, He will give it.

God's Guidance

Lord, You light my lamp; my God illuminates my darkness.
Psalm 18:28 HCSB

The Bible promises that God will guide you if you let Him. Your job, of course, is to let Him. But sometimes, you will be tempted to do otherwise. Sometimes, you'll be tempted to go along with the crowd; other times, you'll be tempted to do things your way, not God's way. When you feel those temptations, resist them.

What will you allow to guide you through the coming day: your own desires (or, for that matter, the desires of your friends)? Or will you allow God to lead the way? The answer should be obvious. You should let God be your guide. When you entrust your life to Him completely and without reservation, God will give you the strength to meet any challenge, the courage to face any trial, and the wisdom to live in His righteousness. So trust Him today and seek His guidance. When you do, your next step will be the right one.

100 QUESTIONS TEENS ASK

Are you serious about wanting God's guidance to become a personal reality in your life? The first step is to tell God that you know you can't manage your own life; that you need his help.

Catherine Marshall

If we want to hear God's voice, we must surrender our minds and hearts to Him.

Billy Graham

Walk in the daylight of God's will because then you will be safe; you will not stumble.

Anne Graham Lotz

It is a joy that God never abandons His children. He guides faithfully all who listen to His directions.

Corrie ten Boom

Enjoy the adventure of receiving God guidance. Taste it, revel in it, appreciate the fact that the journey is often a lot more exciting than arriving at the destination.

Bill Hybels

What does the Bible say about God's love?

THE QUICK ANSWER

God's love makes everything look a lot better: When you invite the love of God into your heart, everything in the world looks different, including you.

God's Love

For the LORD your God has arrived to live among you.
He is a mighty Savior. He will rejoice over you with great gladness.
With his love, he will calm all your fears.
He will exult over you by singing a happy song.
Zephaniah 3:17 NLT

How much does God love you? As long as you're alive, you'll never be able to figure it out because God's love is just too big to comprehend. But this much we know: God loves you so much that He sent His Son Jesus to come to this earth and to die for you! And, when you accepted Jesus into your heart, God gave you a gift that is more precious than gold: the gift of eternal life.

Sometimes, in the crush of your daily duties, God may seem far away, but He is not. God is everywhere you have ever been and everywhere you will ever go. He is with you night and day; He knows your thoughts and your prayers. And, when you earnestly seek Him, you will find Him because He is here, waiting patiently for you to reach out to Him.

St. Augustine observed, "God loves each of us as if there were only one of us." Do you believe those words? Do you seek to have an intimate, one-on-one relationship with your Heavenly Father, or are you satisfied to keep Him at a "safe" distance?

God's love is bigger and more powerful than anybody can imagine, but His love is very real. So do yourself a favor right now: accept God's love with open arms and welcome His Son Jesus into your heart. When you do, your life will be changed today, tomorrow, and forever.

Being loved by Him whose opinion matters most gives us the security to risk loving, too—even loving ourselves.

Gloria Gaither

There is no pit so deep that God's love is not deeper still.

Corrie ten Boom

Even when we cannot see the why and wherefore of God's dealings, we know that there is love in and behind them, so we can rejoice always.

J. I. Packer

Sometimes I'm impatient for life to unfold. What does the Bible say about God's timing?

THE QUICK ANSWER

God has very big plans in store for your life, so trust Him and wait patiently for those plans to unfold. And remember: God's timing is best, so don't allow yourself to become discouraged if things don't work out exactly as you wish. Instead of worrying about your future, entrust it to God. He knows exactly what you need and exactly when you need it.

God's Timing

To everything there is a season,
a time for every purpose under heaven.
Ecclesiastes 3:1 NKJV

We human beings are so impatient. We know what we want, and we know exactly when we want it: RIGHT NOW! But, God knows better. He has created a world that unfolds according to His own timetable, not ours.

As Christians, we must be patient as we wait for God to show us the wonderful plans that He has in store for us. And while we're waiting for God to make His plans clear, let's keep praying and keep giving thanks to the One who has given us more blessings than we can count.

God's silence is in no way indicative of His activity or involvement in our lives. He may be silent, but He is not still.

Charles Swindoll

God has a designated time when his promise will be fulfilled and the prayer will be answered.

Jim Cymbala

Waiting on God brings us to the journey's end quicker than our feet.

Mrs. Charles E. Cowman

When we read of the great Biblical leaders, we see that it was not uncommon for God to ask them to wait, not just a day or two, but for years, until God was ready for them to act.

Gloria Gaither

By his wisdom, he orders his delays so that they prove to be far better than our hurries.

C. H. Spurgeon

QUESTION 54

If I feel guilty about something, what should I do?

THE QUICK ANSWER

If you've asked for God's forgiveness, He has given it. But have you forgiven yourself? If not, the best moment to do so is this one.

Beyond Guilt

Be diligent to present yourself approved to God,
a worker who doesn't need to be ashamed,
correctly teaching the word of truth.
2 Timothy 2:15 HCSB

All of us have made mistakes. Sometimes our failures result from our own shortsightedness. On other occasions, we are swept up in events that are beyond our abilities to control. Under either set of circumstances, we may experience intense feelings of guilt. But God has an answer for the guilt that we feel. That answer, of course, is His forgiveness.

When we ask our Heavenly Father for His forgiveness, He forgives us completely and without reservation. Then, we must do the difficult work of forgiving ourselves in the same way that God has forgiven us: thoroughly and unconditionally.

The Spanish writer Baltasar Gracián noted, "The things we remember best are those better forgotten." If those words describe your thoughts, then it's time for a special kind of housecleaning—a housecleaning of your mind and your heart.

Guilt is a healthy regret for telling God one thing and doing another.

Max Lucado

Spiritual life without guilt would be like physical life without pain. Guilt is a defense mechanism; it's like an alarm that goes off to lead you to confession when you sin.

John MacArthur

If God has forgiven you, why can't you forgive yourself?

Marie T. Freeman

Satan wants you to feel guilty. Your Heavenly Father wants you to know that you are forgiven.

Warren Wiersbe

Guilt is a gift that leads us to grace.

Franklin Graham

2 Timothy 2:15 NCV
Make every effort to give yourself
to God as the kind of person he will
approve. Be a worker who is not ashamed
& who uses the true teaching in the
right way.

Sometimes it's hard to trust God. What does the Bible say about that?

THE QUICK ANSWER

It's simple: depend upon God. Remember the words of Vance Havner: "We must live in all kinds of days, both high days and low days, in simple dependence upon Christ as the branch on the vine. This is the supreme experience."

Trusting God

And God, in his mighty power,
will protect you until you receive this salvation,
because you are trusting him.
1 Peter 1:5 NLT

The journey through life leads us over many peaks and through many valleys. When we reach the mountaintops, we find it easy to praise God, to trust Him, and to give thanks. But, when we trudge through the dark valleys of bitterness and despair, trusting God is more difficult. The next time you find your courage tested to the limit, lean upon God's promises. Trust His Son. When you are worried, anxious, or afraid, call upon Him. God can handle your troubles infinitely better than you can, so turn them over to Him. Remember that God rules both mountaintops and valleys—with limitless wisdom and love—now and forever.

Sometimes the very essence of faith is trusting God in the midst of things He knows good and well we cannot comprehend.

Beth Moore

A prayerful heart and an obedient heart will learn, very slowly and not without sorrow, to stake everything on God Himself.

Elisabeth Elliot

Trusting in my own mental understanding becomes a hindrance to complete trust in God.

Oswald Chambers

God has proven himself as a faithful father. Now it falls to us to be trusting children.

Max Lucado

Never be afraid to trust an unknown future to a known God.

Corrie ten Boom

What does the Bible say about my health?

THE QUICK ANSWER

Do you think God wants you to develop healthy habits? Of course He does! Physical, emotional, and spiritual fitness are all part of God's plan for you. But it's up to you to make certain that a healthy lifestyle is a fundamental part of your plan, too.

Healthy Habits

They brought unto him all sick people that were taken with diverse diseases and torments . . . and he healed them.
Matthew 4:24 KJV

We live in a fast-food world where unhealthy choices are convenient, inexpensive, and tempting. And, we live in a digital world filled with modern conveniences that often rob us of the physical exercise needed to maintain healthy lifestyles. As a result, too many of us find ourselves glued to the television, with a snack in one hand and a clicker in the other. The results are as unfortunate as they are predictable.

Would you like to improve your physical health? If so, start by taking personal responsibility for the body that God has given you. Then, make the solemn pledge to yourself that you will begin to make the changes that are required to enjoy a longer, healthier, happier life. No one can make those changes for you; you must make them for yourself. And with God's help, you can . . . and you will.

A Christian should no more defile his body than a Jew would defile the temple.

Warren Wiersbe

You can't buy good health at the doctor's office—you've got to earn it for yourself.

Marie T. Freeman

If you desire to improve your physical well-being and your emotional outlook, increasing your faith can help you.

John Maxwell

Laughter is the language of the young at heart and the antidote to what ails us.

Barbara Johnson

QUESTION 57

Plenty of people could use a helping hand. What does the Bible instruct us to do about it?

THE QUICK ANSWER

Feel better about yourself by helping other people. When talking to other people, ask yourself this question: "How helpful can I be?" When you help others, you'll be proud of yourself, and God will be, too!

Helping Others

Then a Samaritan—traveling down the road came to where t he hurt man was. When he saw the man, he felt very sorry for him. The Samaritan went to him, poured olive oil and wine—on his wounds, and bandaged them. Then he put the hurt man on his own donkey and took him to an inn where he cared for him.
Luke 10:33-34 NCV

Jesus told the story of the "Good Samaritan," a man who helped a fellow traveler when no one else would. We, too, should be good Samaritans when we find people who need our help.

Zora Neale Hurston noted, "When you find a man who has lost his way, you don't make fun of him and scorn him and leave him there. You show him the way. If you don't do that you just prove that you're sort of lost yourself."

And Helen Keller advised, "Believe, when you are most unhappy, that there is something for you to do in the world. So long as you can sweeten another's pain, life is not in vain."

So today, find somebody who needs a hug or a helping hand . . . and give them both.

Encouraging others means helping people, looking for the best in them, and trying to bring out their positive qualities.

John Maxwell

Do all the good you can. By all the means you can. In all the ways you can. In all the places you can. At all the times you can. To all the people you can. As long as ever you can.

John Wesley

You cannot cure your sorrow by nursing it; but you can cure it by nursing another's sorrow.

George Matheson

Make it a rule, and pray to God to help you to keep it, never, if possible, to lie down at night without being able to say: "I have made one human being at least a little wiser, or a little happier, or at least a little better this day."

Charles Kingsley

Sometimes the truth hurts. What does the Bible say about honesty?

THE QUICK ANSWER

Little white lies? Beware! You may think that there's a big difference between "little" lies and king-sized ones. Unfortunately, little white lies have a tendency to grow into big trouble . . . in a hurry.

The Best Policy

The just man walketh in his integrity:
his children are blessed after him.
Proverbs 20:7 KJV

Maybe you've heard this familiar phrase: "Honesty is the best policy." But, honesty is not just the best policy; it is also God's policy.

An important part of becoming a good person is learning to tell the truth. Lies usually have a way of hurting people, so even when it's hard, we must be honest with others.

If we are going to follow the rules that God has given us, we must remember that truth is not just the best way; it is also His way.

The single most important element in any human relationship is honesty—with oneself, with God, and with others.

Catherine Marshall

Honesty has a beautiful and refreshing simplicity about it. No ulterior motives. No hidden meanings. As honesty and integrity characterize our lives, there will be no need to manipulate others.

Charles Swindoll

The commandment of absolute truthfulness is really only another name for the fullness of discipleship.

Dietrich Bonhoeffer

You cannot glorify Christ and practice deception at the same time.

Warren Wiersbe

God doesn't expect you to be perfect, but he does insist on complete honesty.

Rick Warren

Sometimes it's hard to be hopeful. What does the Bible say about hope?

THE QUICK ANSWER

Don't give up hope: Other people have experienced the same kind of hard times you may be experiencing now. They made it, and so can you (Psalm 146:5).

Finding Hope

Let us hold on to the confession of our hope without wavering,
for He who promised is faithful.
Hebrews 10:23 HCSB

There are few sadder sights on earth than the sight of a girl or guy who has lost hope. In difficult times, hope can be elusive, but those who place their faith in God's promises need never lose it. After all, God is good; His love endures; He has promised His children the gift of eternal life. And, God keeps His promises.

Despite God's promises, despite Christ's love, and despite our countless blessings, we're only human, and we can still lose hope from time to time. When we do, we need the encouragement of Christian friends, the life-changing power of prayer, and the healing truth of God's Holy Word.

If you find yourself falling into the spiritual traps of worry and discouragement, seek the healing touch of Jesus and the encouraging words of fellow believers. And if you find a friend in need, remind him or her of the peace that is found through a genuine relationship with Christ. It was Christ who promised, "I have told you these things so that in Me you may have peace. In the world you have suffering. But take courage! I have conquered the world" (John 16:33 HCSB). This world can be a place of trials and troubles, but as believers, we are secure. God has promised us peace, joy, and eternal life. And, of course, God keeps His promises today, tomorrow, and forever.

———————————————

Never yield to gloomy anticipation. Place your hope and confidence in God. He has no record of failure.

Mrs. Charles E. Cowman

The best we can hope for in this life is a knothole peek at the shining realities ahead. Yet a glimpse is enough. It's enough to convince our hearts that whatever sufferings and sorrows currently assail us aren't worthy of comparison to that which waits over the horizon.

Joni Eareckson Tada

Faith looks back and draws courage; hope looks ahead and keeps desire alive.

John Eldredge

QUESTION 60

What does God's Word say about God's Son?

THE QUICK ANSWER

What a friend you have in Jesus: Jesus loves you, and He offers you eternal life with Him in heaven. Welcome Him into your heart. Now!

What a Friend

In the beginning was the Word, and the Word was with God, and the Word was God.... And the Word was made flesh, and dwelt among us, (and we beheld his glory, the glory as of the only begotten of the Father,) full of grace and truth.
John 1:1, 14 KJV

The 19th-century writer Hannah Whitall Smith observed, "The crucial question for each of us is this: What do you think of Jesus, and do you yet have a personal acquaintance with Him?" Indeed, the answer to that question determines the quality, the course, and the direction of our lives today and for all eternity.

The old familiar hymn begins, "What a friend we have in Jesus . . . ." No truer words were ever penned. Jesus is the sovereign Friend and ultimate Savior of mankind. Christ showed enduring love for His believers by willingly sacrificing His own life so that we might have eternal life. Now, it is our turn to become His friend.

Let us love our Savior, praise Him, and share His message of salvation with our neighbors and with the world. When we do, we demonstrate that our acquaintance with the Master is not a passing fancy; it is, instead, the cornerstone and the touchstone of our lives.

———————————

His name blossoms on the pages of history like the flowers of a thousand springtimes in one bouquet.

R. G. Lee

When we are in a situation where Jesus is all we have, we soon discover he is all we really need.

Gigi Graham Tchividjian

The only source of Life is the Lord Jesus Christ.

Oswald Chambers

In your greatest weakness, turn to your greatest strength, Jesus, and hear Him say, "My grace is sufficient for you, for My strength is made perfect in weakness" (2 Corinthians 12:9, NKJV).

Lisa Whelchel

What does the Bible have to say about the importance of being a joyful person?

THE QUICK ANSWER

Joy does not depend upon your circumstances, but upon your relationship with God.

Real Joy

These things I have spoken to you, that My joy may remain in you, and that your joy may be full.
John 15:11 NKJV

Have you made the choice to rejoice? Hopefully so. After all, if you're a believer, you have plenty of reasons to be joyful. Yet sometimes, amid the inevitable hustle and bustle of life here on earth, you may lose sight of your blessings as you wrestle with the challenges of everyday life.

Christ made it clear to His followers: He intended that His joy would become their joy. And it still holds true today: Christ intends that His believers share His love with His joy in their hearts.

What does life have in store for you? A world full of possibilities (of course it's up to you to seize them), and God's promise of abundance (of course it's up to you to accept it). So, as you embark upon the next phase of your journey, remember to celebrate the life that God has given you. Your Creator has blessed you beyond measure. Honor Him with your prayers, your words, your deeds, and your joy.

I choose joy. I will refuse the temptation to be cynical; cynicism is the tool of a lazy thinker. I will refuse to see people as anything less than human beings, created by God. I will refuse to see any problem as anything less than an opportunity to see God.

Max Lucado

A life of intimacy with God is characterized by joy.

Oswald Chambers

Some of us seem so anxious about avoiding hell that we forget to celebrate our journey toward heaven.

Philip Yancey

The Christian should be an alleluia from head to foot!

St. Augustine

The Christian lifestyle is not one of legalistic do's and don'ts, but one that is positive, attractive, and joyful.

Vonette Bright

It's hard not to be judgmental of other people, and it's hard not to judge their motives. What does the Bible say about judging others?

THE QUICK ANSWER

Your ability to judge others requires a divine insight that you simply don't have. So do everybody (including yourself) a favor: don't judge.

Let God Judge

Speak and act as those who will be judged by the law of freedom.
For judgment is without mercy to the one who hasn't shown mercy.
Mercy triumphs over judgment.
James 2:12-13 HCSB

Would you like a surefire formula for being unhappy? Here it is: spend as much time as you can judging other people. But if you'd rather be happy—and if you'd rather guard your heart by obeying your Heavenly Father—please remember this: in matters of judgment, God certainly does not need your help. Why? Because God is perfectly capable of judging the human heart . . . while you are not.

God is perfect; we are not. So none of us are qualified to "cast the first stone." Thankfully, God has forgiven us, and we, too, must forgive others. It's just not that complicated!

Have you developed the bad habit of behaving yourself like an amateur judge and jury, assigning blame and condemnation wherever you go? If so, it's time to grow up and obey God. When it comes to judging everything and everybody, God doesn't need your help . . . and He doesn't want it.

An individual Christian may see fit to give up all sorts of things for special reasons—marriage or meat or beer or cinema; but the moment he starts saying these things are bad in themselves, or looking down his nose at other people who do use them, he has taken the wrong turn.

C. S. Lewis

Don't judge other people more harshly than you want God to judge you.

Marie T. Freeman

No creed or school of thought can monopolize the Spirit of God.

Oswald Chambers

Christians think they are prosecuting attorneys or judges, when, in reality, God has called all of us to be witnesses.

Warren Wiersbe

I know I should be kind to other people, but sometimes it's so easy to overlook the needs of others. What does the Bible instruct me to do?

THE QUICK ANSWER

You can't just talk about it: In order to be a kind person, you must not only think kind thoughts; you must also do kind things. So get busy! The best day to become a more generous person is this day!

Kindness Is a Choice

Show respect for all people.
Love the brothers and sisters of God's family.
1 Peter 2:17 ICB

Christ showed His love for us by willingly sacrificing His own life so that we might have eternal life: "But God demonstrates his own love for us in this: While we were still sinners, Christ died for us" (Romans 5:8 NIV). We, as Christ's followers, are challenged to share His love with kind words on our lips and praise in our hearts.

Just as Christ has been—and will always be—the ultimate friend to His flock, so should we be Christlike in the kindness and generosity that we show toward others, especially those who are most in need.

When we walk each day with Jesus—and obey the commandments found in God's Holy Word—we become worthy ambassadors for Christ. When we share the love of Christ, we share a priceless gift with the world. As His servants, we must do no less.

When you extend hospitality to others, you're not trying to impress people, you're trying to reflect God to them.

Max Lucado

Do all the good you can. By all the means you can. In all the ways you can. In all the places you can. At all the times you can. To all the people you can. As long as you can.

John Wesley

The mark of a Christian is that he will walk the second mile and turn the other cheek. A wise man or woman gives the extra effort, all for the glory of the Lord Jesus Christ.

John Maxwell

There are many timid souls whom we jostle morning and evening as we pass them by; but if only the kind word were spoken they might become fully persuaded.

Fanny Crosby

What does the Bible say about listening to God?

THE QUICK ANSWER

When you're communicating with God, try to listen more and talk less.

Listening to God

*God has no use for the prayers of the people
who won't listen to him.*
Proverbs 28:9 MSG

God's Word instructs us to be quick to listen and slow to speak. And when it comes to the important job of encouraging our friends and family members, we're wise to listen carefully (first) and then offer helpful words (next).

Perhaps God gave us two ears and one mouth for a reason: so that we might listen twice as much as we speak. After all, listening quietly to another person can sometimes be a wonderful form of encouragement. Besides, after you've listened carefully to the other guy (or girl), you're twice as likely to speak wisely, not impulsively.

Today and every day, you have the power to comfort others with your words and your ears . . . with an emphasis on the latter.

And sometimes, the words you don't speak are just as helpful as the ones you do speak. So talk—and listen—accordingly.

When we come to Jesus stripped of pretensions, with a needy spirit, ready to listen, He meets us at the point of need.

Catherine Marshall

In the soul-searching of our lives, we are to stay quiet so we can hear Him say all that He wants to say to us in our hearts.

Charles Swindoll

We cannot experience the fullness of Christ if we do all the expressing. We must allow God to express His love, will, and truth to us.

Gary Smalley

Be quiet enough to hear God's whisper.

Anonymous

It is in that stillness that the Voice will be heard, the only voice in all the universe that speaks peace to the deepest part of us.

Elisabeth Elliot

When I'm lonely, what should I do? What does the Bible say about loneliness?

THE QUICK ANSWER

Lonely? God is close by, and so is someone who needs your help. If you find someone to help, you won't be lonely for long.

When You're Lonely

Have I not commanded you? Be strong and of good courage;
do not be afraid, nor be dismayed,
for the Lord your God is with you wherever you go.
Joshua 1:9 NKJV

If you're like most people, you've experienced occasional bouts of loneliness. If so, you understand the genuine pain that accompanies those feelings that "nobody cares." In truth, lots of people care about you, but at times, you may hardly notice their presence.

Sometimes, intense feelings of loneliness can be the result of depression. Other times, however, your feelings of loneliness come as a result of your own hesitation: the hesitation to get out there and make new friends.

The world is literally teeming with people who are looking for new friends. And yet, ironically enough, too many of us allow our friendships to wither away, not because we intentionally alienate others, but because we simply don't pay enough attention to them.

Ralph Waldo Emerson advised, "The only way to have a friend is to be one." Emerson realized that a lasting relationship, like a beautiful garden, must be tended with care. Here are a few helpful tips on tending the garden of friendship . . . and reaping a bountiful harvest: 1. Remember the first rule of friendship: it's the Golden one, and it starts like this: "Do unto others . . ." (Matthew 7:12). 2. If you're trying to make new friends, become interested in them . . . and eventually they'll become interested in you (Colossians 3:12). 3. Take the time to reconnect with old friends: they'll be glad you did, and so, too, will you (Philippians 1:3). 4. Become more involved in your church or in community service: they'll welcome your participation, and you'll welcome the chance to connect with more and more people (1 Peter 5:2).

We are born helpless. As soon as we are fully conscious we discover loneliness. We need others physically, emotionally, intellectually; we need them if we are to know anything, even ourselves.

C. S. Lewis

What does the Bible say about love?

THE QUICK ANSWER

Love at first sight always deserves a second look: If you give your heart away too easily or too often, you may find that it is returned you . . . in very poor condition!

Love According to God

If I speak the languages of men and of angels, but do not have love,
I am a sounding gong or a clanging cymbal.
1 Corinthians 13:1 HCSB

If you're trying to build a relationship based only on physical attraction, you'll be disappointed. Lasting relationships aren't built upon lust; they're built upon love—real love.

How do you define love? Hopefully, you understand that it's something more than physical attraction. Genuine love is patient, understanding, consistent, and considerate. Genuine love doesn't just sit around and do nothing; it gets translated into acts of kindness—both large and small.

Love is always a choice. Sometimes, of course, we may "fall in love," but it takes work to stay there. Sometimes, we may be "swept off our feet," but the "sweeping" is only temporary;

sooner or later, if love is to endure, one must plant one's feet firmly on the ground. The decision to love another person for a lifetime is much more than the simple process of "falling in" or "being swept up." It requires "reaching out," "holding firm," and "lifting up." Love, then, becomes a decision to honor and care for the other person, come what may.

———————————————

Those who abandon ship the first time it enters a storm miss the calm beyond. And the rougher the storms weathered together, the deeper and stronger real love grows.

Ruth Bell Graham

How do you spell love? When you reach the point where the happiness, security, and development of another person is as much of a driving force to you as your own happiness, security, and development, then you have a mature love. True love is spelled G-I-V-E. It is not based on what you can get, but rooted in what you can give to the other person.

Josh McDowell

Love must be supported and fed and protected, just like a little infant who is growing up at home.

James Dobson

What does the Bible say about the love and reverence I should feel for God?

THE QUICK ANSWER

Express yourself! If you sincerely love God, don't be too bashful to tell Him so. And while you're at it, don't be too bashful to tell other people about your feelings. If you love God, say so!

Loving God

He said to him, "You shall love the Lord your God with all your heart, with all your soul, and with all your mind. This is the greatest and most important commandment."
Matthew 22:37-38 HCSB

C. S. Lewis observed, "A person's spiritual health is exactly proportional to his love for God." If we are to enjoy the spiritual health that God intends for us, we should keep Lewis's words in mind.

Corrie ten Boom noted, "A bird does not know it can fly before it uses its wings. We learn God's love in our hearts as soon as we act upon it." She understood that whenever we worship God with our hearts and our minds, we are blessed by our love for Him and His love for us.

Today, open your heart to the Father. And let your obedience be a fitting response to His never-ending love.

Whatever you love most, be it sports, pleasure, business or God, that is your god.

Billy Graham

Joy is a by-product not of happy circumstances, education or talent, but of a healthy relationship with God and a determination to love Him no matter what.

Barbara Johnson

When we develop an authentic love relationship with God, we will not be able to keep Him compartmentalized in "churchy," religious categories.

Beth Moore

Telling the Lord how much you love Him and why is what praise and worship are all about.

Lisa Whelchel

What is Christian perfection? Loving God with all our heart, mind, soul, and strength.

John Wesley

We live in a materialistic world. What does the Bible have to say about that?

THE QUICK ANSWER

Too much stuff doesn't ensure happiness. In fact, having too much stuff can actually prevent happiness.

Beyond Materialism

And He told them, "Watch out and be on guard against all greed, because one's life is not in the abundance of his possessions."
Luke 12:15 HCSB

Is "shop till you drop" your motto? Hopefully not. On the grand stage of a well-lived life, material possessions should play a rather small role. Of course, we all need the basic necessities of life, but once we meet those needs, the piling up of stuff creates more problems than it solves.

Our society is in love with money and the things that money can buy. God is not. God cares about people, not possessions, and so must we. We must, to the best of our abilities, love our neighbors as ourselves, and we must, to the best of our abilities, resist the mighty temptation to place possessions ahead of people.

How much stuff is too much stuff? Well, if your desire for stuff is getting in the way of your desire to know God, then you've got too much stuff—it's as simple as that.

If you find yourself wrapped up in the concerns of the material world, it's time to reorder your priorities by turning your thoughts to more important matters. And, it's time to begin storing up riches that will endure throughout eternity: the spiritual kind. Money, in and of itself, is not evil; worshipping money is. So today, as you prioritize matters of importance in your life, remember that God is almighty, but the dollar is not.

A society that pursues pleasure runs the risk of raising expectations ever higher, so that true contentment always lies tantalizingly out of reach.

Philip Yancey and Paul Brand

If you want to be truly happy, you won't find it on an endless quest for more stuff. You'll find it in receiving God's generosity and in the passing that generosity along.

Bill Hybels

The Scriptures also reveal warning that if we are consumed with greed, not only do we disobey God, but we will miss the opportunity to allow Him to use us as instruments for others.

Charles Stanley

What does the Bible have to teach me about maturity?

THE QUICK ANSWER

God is still working in you and through you. Even if you're a mature Christian, you can still grow in the knowledge and love of your Savior every day that you live.

Growing Up

When I was a child, I spoke and thought and reasoned as a child does. But when I grew up, I put away childish things.
1 Corinthians 13:11 NLT

The journey toward spiritual maturity lasts a lifetime. As Christians, we can and should continue to grow in the love and the knowledge of our Savior as long as we live. Norman Vincent Peale had the following advice for believers of all ages: "Ask the God who made you to keep remaking you." That advice, of course, is perfectly sound, but often ignored.

When we cease to grow, either emotionally or spiritually, we do ourselves a profound disservice. But, if we study God's Word, if we obey His commandments, and if we live in the center of His will, we will not be "stagnant" believers; we will, instead, be growing Christians . . . and that's exactly what God intends for us to be.

Life is a series of choices and decisions. Each day, we make countless decisions that can bring us closer to God . . . or not. When we live according to the principles contained in God's Holy Word, we embark upon a journey of spiritual maturity that results in life abundant and life eternal.

We set our eyes on the finish line, forgetting the past, and straining toward the mark of spiritual maturity and fruitfulness.

Vonette Bright

You are either becoming more like Christ every day or you're becoming less like Him. There is no neutral position in the Lord.

Stormie Omartian

The vigor of our spiritual lives will be in exact proportion to the place held by the Bible in our lives and in our thoughts.

George Mueller

God's plan for our guidance is for us to grow gradually in wisdom before we get to the crossroads.

Bill Hybels

What does the Bible say about mentors?

THE QUICK ANSWER

Rely on the advice of trusted friends and mentors. Proverbs 1:5 makes it clear: "A wise man will hear and increase learning, and a man of understanding will attain wise counsel" (NKJV).

Finding the Right Mentors

The way of a fool is right in his own eyes,
but he who heeds counsel is wise.
Proverbs 12:15 NKJV

Would you like to become a little wiser? Or maybe a lot wiser? If so, then you should make it a point to surround yourself with people who, by their words and their presence, make you a smarter person. But it doesn't stop there. You should also work overtime to avoid hanging out with anybody who encourages you to think foolish thoughts or do foolish things.

Whenever you ask people for advice, it's smart to ask folks who have been there, and done that. So, if you want to get real smart real fast, you'll find thoughtful, mature adults who can help you chart your course through life.

100 QUESTIONS TEENS ASK

Today, as a gift to yourself, select—from your friends, teachers, or family members—at least two mentors whose judgment you trust. Then listen carefully to your mentors' advice and be willing to accept that advice, even if accepting it requires effort or pain, or both. Consider your mentors to be God's gifts to you. Thank God for those gifts, and use them.

Yes, the Spirit was sent to be our Counselor. Yes, Jesus speaks to us personally. But often he works through another human being.

John Eldredge

The effective mentor strives to help a man or woman discover what they can be in Christ and then holds them accountable to become that person.

Howard Hendricks

It takes a wise person to give good advice, but an even wiser person to take it.

Marie T. Freeman

A single word, if spoken in a friendly spirit, may be sufficient to turn one from dangerous error.

Fanny Crosby

It's hard for me to believe in miracles. What assurances can I find in the Bible?

THE QUICK ANSWER

If you're looking for miracles . . . you'll find them. If you're not, you won't.

Do You Believe in Miracles?

Is anything impossible for the Lord?
Genesis 18:14 HCSB

If you haven't seen any of God's miracles lately, you haven't been looking. Throughout history, the Creator has intervened in the course of human events in ways that cannot be explained by science or human rationale. And He's still doing so today.

God's miracles are not limited to special occasions, nor are they witnessed by a select few. God is crafting His wonders all around us: the miracle of the birth of a new baby, the miracle of a world renewing itself with every sunrise, the miracle of lives transformed by God's love and grace. Each day, God's handiwork is evident for all to see and experience.

100 QUESTIONS TEENS ASK

Today, seize the opportunity to inspect God's hand at work. His miracles come in a variety of shapes and sizes, so keep your eyes and your heart open. Be watchful, and you'll soon be amazed.

I could go through this day oblivious to the miracles all around me or I could tune in and "enjoy."

Gloria Gaither

The miracles in fact are a retelling in small letters of the very same story which is written across the whole world in letters too large for some of us to see.

C. S. Lewis

When God is involved, anything can happen. Be open and stay that way. God has a beautiful way of bringing good vibrations out of broken chords.

Charles Swindoll

When we face an impossible situation, all self-reliance and self-confidence must melt away; we must be totally dependent on Him for the resources.

Anne Graham Lotz

What does the Bible say about missions?

THE QUICK ANSWER

God will empower you to share your faith.

Sharing Your Faith

Now then we are ambassadors for Christ . . . .
2 Corinthians 5:20 KJV

After His resurrection, Jesus addressed His disciples:

But the eleven disciples proceeded to Galilee, to the mountain which Jesus had designated. When they saw Him, they worshiped Him; but some were doubtful. And Jesus came up and spoke to them, saying, "All authority has been given to Me in heaven and on earth. Go therefore and make disciples of all the nations, baptizing them in the name of the Father and the Son and the Holy Spirit, teaching them to observe all that I commanded you; and lo, I am with you always, even to the end of the age." (Matthew 28:16–20 NASB)

Christ's great commission applies to Christians of every generation, including our own. As believers, we are called to share the Good News of Jesus Christ with our families, with our neighbors, and with the world. Jesus commanded His disciples to become fishers of men. We must do likewise, and we must do so today. Tomorrow may indeed be too late.

———————————————

Taking the gospel to people wherever they are—death row, the ghetto, or next door—is frontline evangelism, frontline love. It is our one hope for breaking down barriers and for restoring the sense of community, of caring for one another, that our decadent, impersonalized culture has sucked out of us.

Chuck Colson

Our commission is quite specific. We are told to be His witness to all nations. For us, as His disciples, to refuse any part of this commission frustrates the love of Jesus Christ, the Son of God.

Catherine Marshall

We are now, a very, very few feeble workers, scattering the grain broadcast according as time and strength permit. God will give the harvest; doubt it not. But the laborers are few.

Lottie Moon

Missions is God finding those whose hearts are right with Him and placing them where they can make a difference for His kingdom.

Henry Blackaby

I've made mistakes. What should I do?

THE QUICK ANSWER

Made a mistake? Ask for forgiveness! If you've broken one of God's rules, you can always ask Him for His forgiveness. And He will always give it!

Beyond the Mistakes

*Flee from youthful passions, and pursue righteousness,
faith, love, and peace, along with those who
call on the Lord from a pure heart.*
2 Timothy 2:22 HCSB

Mistakes: nobody likes 'em but everybody makes 'em. And you're no different! When you commit the inevitable blunders of life (and you will), do your best to correct them, learn from them, and pray for the wisdom to avoid those same mistakes in the future. If you're successful, the missteps of today will become the stepping stones of tomorrow. And your life will become a non-stop learning experience.

Mistakes are the price you pay for being human; repeated mistakes are the price you pay for being stubborn. So don't be hardheaded: learn from your experiences—the first time!

No matter how badly we have failed, we can always get up and begin again. Our God is the God of new beginnings.

Warren Wiersbe

God is able to take mistakes, when they are committed to Him, and make of them something for our good and for His glory.

Ruth Bell Graham

There is nothing wrong with asking God's direction. But it is wrong to go our own way, then expect Him to bail us out.

Larry Burkett

Mistakes offer the possibility for redemption and a new start in God's kingdom. No matter what you're guilty of, God can restore your innocence.

Barbara Johnson

Truth will sooner come out of error than from confusion.

Francis Bacon

It isn't easy to be a moderate person. What should I do?

THE QUICK ANSWER

Adopt healthy habits that you can stick with. In other words, don't starve yourself. Be moderate, even in your moderation.

The Wisdom of Moderation

An overseer, then, must be above reproach,
the husband of one wife, temperate, prudent, respectable,
hospitable, able to teach, not addicted to wine or pugnacious,
but gentle, peaceable, free from the love of money.
1 Timothy 3:2-3 NASB

Would you like to improve—dramatically improve—the quality of your life? Then here's a simple, time-tested formula: learn to harness your appetites and to restrain your impulses. In other words, learn the wisdom of moderation.

When we learn to temper our appetites, our desires, and our impulses, we are blessed, in part, because God has created a world in which temperance is rewarded and intemperance is inevitably punished.

Moderation is difficult, of course; it is especially difficult in a prosperous society such as ours. But the rewards of moderation are numerous and long-lasting. Claim those rewards today. No one can force you to moderate your appetites. The decision to live temperately (and wisely) is yours and yours alone. And so are the consequences.

When I feel like circumstances are spiraling downward in my life, God taught me that whether I'm right side up or upside down, I need to turn those circumstances over to Him. He is the only one who can bring balance into my life.

Carole Lewis

Virtue—even attempted virtue—brings light; indulgence brings fog.

C. S. Lewis

I discipline my body and make it my slave.

1 Corinthians 9:27 NASB

No one can serve two masters; for either he will hate the one and love the other, or he will be devoted to one and despise the other. You cannot serve God and wealth.

Matthew 6:24 NASB

Sometimes it's hard to be an obedient Christian. What does the Bible say about obedience?

THE QUICK ANSWER

Obey God or face the consequences: God rewards obedience and punishes disobedience. It's not enough to understand God's rules; you must also live by them . . . or else.

Obedience Now

I have sought You with all my heart;
don't let me wander from Your commands.
Psalm 119:10 HCSB

Ours is a noisy, troubled world, a world in which peace can be a scarce commodity—but it need not be so. The Bible promises that peace can be ours when we trust God's promises and obey His commandments. But the Bible also issues a warning: If we pay scant attention to God's Word, or if we rebel against His teachings altogether, we may forfeit countless blessings that might otherwise have been ours.

Would you like to enjoy the genuine, lasting peace that only God can provide? Then study His Word and honor Him with your actions. When you do, you'll soon discover that obedience is the path to peace. It always has been, and it always will be.

The cross that Jesus commands you and me to carry is the cross of submissive obedience to the will of God, even when His will includes suffering and hardship and things we don't want to do.

Anne Graham Lotz

True faith commits us to obedience.

A. W. Tozer

You may not always see immediate results, but all God wants is your obedience and faithfulness.

Vonette Bright

I don't always like His decisions, but when I choose to obey Him, the act of obedience still "counts" with Him even if I'm not thrilled about it.

Beth Moore

Trials and sufferings teach us to obey the Lord by faith, and we soon learn that obedience pays off in joyful ways.

Bill Bright

What does the Bible say about optimism?

THE QUICK ANSWER

Be a realistic optimist. Your attitude toward the future will help create your future. You might as well put the self-fulfilling prophecy to work for you, and besides, life is far too short to be a pessimist.

Optimism Now

Make me to hear joy and gladness . . . .
Psalm 51:8 KJV

Face facts: pessimism and Christianity don't mix. Why? Because Christians have every reason to be optimistic about life here on earth and life eternal. Mrs. Charles E. Cowman advised, "Never yield to gloomy anticipation. Place your hope and confidence in God. He has no record of failure."

Sometimes, despite our trust in God, we may fall into the spiritual traps of worry, frustration, anxiety, or sheer exhaustion, and our hearts become heavy. What's needed is plenty of rest, a large dose of perspective, and God's healing touch, but not necessarily in that order.

Today, make this promise to yourself and keep it: vow to be a hope-filled Christian. Think optimistically about your life, your education, your family, and your future. Trust your hopes, not your fears. Take time to celebrate God's glorious creation. And then, when you've filled your heart with hope, share your optimism with others. They'll be better for it, and so will you. But not necessarily in that order.

The people whom I have seen succeed best in life have always been cheerful and hopeful people who went about their business with a smile on their faces.

Charles Kingsley

The Christian lifestyle is not one of legalistic do's and don'ts, but one that is positive, attractive, and joyful.

Vonette Bright

We may run, walk, stumble, drive, or fly, but let us never lose sight of the reason for the journey, or miss a chance to see a rainbow on the way.

Gloria Gaither

If you can't tell whether your glass is half-empty or half-full, you don't need another glass; what you need is better eyesight . . . and a more thankful heart.

Marie T. Freeman

How does the Bible instruct me to treat my parents?

THE QUICK ANSWER

You don't have to haul your parents to a deserted island to have a meaningful conversation. Meaningful moments between you and your parents can happen anywhere—give it a try.

Listen to Your Parents

Honor your father and your mother so that you may have a long life in the land that the Lord your God is giving you.
Exodus 20:12 HCSB

Directions, directions, directions. It seems like people (usually your parents) are always giving you directions: telling you where to go, how to behave, and what to do next. And whether you like it or not, your parents are usually right.

If you're like most young people, you may, from time to time, resist the advice you receive from your mom or dad. But don't resist too much. Your parents usually know what's best. And if you're smart, you'll listen to them.

The child that never learns to obey his parents in the home will not obey God or man out of the home.

Susanna Wesley

Let us look upon our children; let us love them and train them as children of the covenant and children of the promise. These are the children of God.

Andrew Murray

Perfect parents don't exist, but a perfect God does.

Beth Moore

Your children learn more of your faith during the bad times than they do during the good times.

Beverly LaHaye

Children miss nothing in sizing up their parents. If you are only half-convinced of your beliefs, they will quickly discern that fact.

James Dobson

Sometimes it's hard to be patient. What advice can I find in God's Word?

THE QUICK ANSWER

Henry Blackaby writes, "The grass that is here today and gone tomorrow does not require much time to mature. A big oak tree that lasts for generations requires much more time to grow and mature. God is concerned about your life through eternity. Allow Him to take all the time He needs to shape you for His purposes. Larger assignments will require longer periods of preparation." How true!

The Power of Patience

Patience is better than strength.
Proverbs 16:32 ICB

Most of us are impatient for God to grant us the desires of our heart. Usually, we know what we want, and we know precisely when we want it: right now, if not sooner. But God may have other plans. And when God's plans differ from our own, we must trust in His infinite wisdom and in His infinite love.

As busy guys and gals living in a fast-paced world, many of us find that waiting quietly for God is difficult. Why? Because we are imperfect human beings seeking to live according to our own timetables, not God's. In our better moments, we realize that patience is not only a virtue, but it is also a commandment from the Creator.

God instructs us to be patient in all things. We must be patient with our families, with our friends, and with our acquaintances. We must also be patient with our Heavenly Father as He unfolds His plan for our lives. And that's as it should be. After all, think how patient God has been with us.

Waiting is an essential part of spiritual discipline. It can be the ultimate test of faith.

Anne Graham Lotz

The next time you're disappointed, don't panic. Don't give up. Just be patient and let God remind you he's still in control.

Max Lucado

He makes us wait. He keeps us in the dark on purpose. He makes us walk when we want to run, sit still when we want to walk, for he has things to do in our souls that we are not interested in.

Elisabeth Elliot

Peer pressure is everywhere. What should I do?

THE QUICK ANSWER

Face facts: Since you can't please everybody, you're better off trying to please God.

Beyond Peer Pressure

Friend, don't go along with evil. Model the good.
The person who does good does God's work.
The person who does evil falsifies God,
doesn't know the first thing about God.
3 John 1:11 MSG

Our world is filled with pressures: some good, some bad. The pressures that we feel to follow God's will and to behave responsibly are positive pressures. God places them on our hearts, and He intends that we act accordingly. But we also face different pressures, ones that are definitely not from God. When we feel pressured to do things—or even to think thoughts—that lead us away from God, we must beware.

Society seeks to mold us into the cookie-cutter images that are the product of the modern media. God seeks to mold us into new beings, new creations through Christ, beings that are most certainly not conformed to this world. If we are to please God, we must resist the pressures that society seeks to impose upon us, and we must conform ourselves, instead, to His will, to His path, and to His Son.

We, as God's people, are not only to stay far away from sin and sinners who would entice us, but we are to be so like our God that we mourn over sin.

Kay Arthur

You will get untold flak for prioritizing God's revealed and present will for your life over man's . . . but, boy, is it worth it.

Beth Moore

Comparison is the root of all feelings of inferiority.

James Dobson

Those who follow the crowd usually get lost in it.

Rick Warren

Do you want to be wise? Choose wise friends.

Charles Swindoll

QUESTION 80

What does the Bible say about perfectionism?

THE QUICK ANSWER

Don't be too hard on yourself: you don't have to be perfect to be wonderful.

Beyond Perfectionism

The fear of human opinion disables;
trusting in God protects you from that.
Proverbs 29:25 MSG

When God made you, He equipped you with an array of talents and abilities that are uniquely yours. It's up to you to discover those talents and to use them, but sometimes your own perfectionism may get in the way.

If you're your own worst critic, give it up. After all, God doesn't expect you to be perfect, and if that's okay with Him, then it should be okay with you, too.

When you accepted Christ as your Savior, God accepted you for all eternity. Now, it's your turn to accept yourself. When you do, you'll feel a tremendous weight being lifted from your shoulders. And that's as it should be. After all, only one earthly being ever lived life to perfection, and He was the Son of God.

The rest of us have fallen short of God's standard and need to be accepting of our own limitations as well as the limitations of others.

I want you to remember what a difference there is between perfection and perfectionism. The former is a Bible truth; the latter may or may not be a human perversion of the truth. I fear that many, in their horror of perfectionism, reject perfection too.

Andrew Murray

The happiest people in the world are not those who have no problems, but the people who have learned to live with those things that are less than perfect.

James Dobson

God is so inconceivably good. He's not looking for perfection. He already saw it in Christ. He's looking for affection.

Beth Moore

What makes a Christian a Christian is not perfection but forgiveness.

Max Lucado

Sometimes I'm tempted to give up. What advice does the Bible have for me?

THE QUICK ANSWER

The world encourages instant gratification but God's work takes time. Remember the words of C. H. Spurgeon: "By perseverance, the snail reached the ark."

The Power of Perseverance

For you need endurance, so that after you have done God's will, you may receive what was promised.
Hebrews 10:36 HCSB

Are you one of those people who doesn't give up easily, or are you quick to bail out when the going gets tough? If you've developed the unfortunate habit of giving up at the first sign of trouble, it's probably time for you to have a heart-to-heart talk with the person you see every time you look in the mirror.

A well-lived life is like a marathon, not a sprint—it calls for preparation, determination, and lots of perseverance. As an example of perfect perseverance, you need look no further than your Savior, Jesus Christ.

Jesus finished what He began, and so should you. Christ was unwavering in His faithfulness to God. You, too, should remain faithful, especially when times are tough.

Are you facing a difficult situation? If so, remember this: whatever your problem, God can handle it. Your job is to keep persevering until He does.

Keep adding, keep walking, keep advancing; do not stop, do not turn back, do not turn from the straight road.

St. Augustine

In the Bible, patience is not a passive acceptance of circumstances. It is a courageous perseverance in the face of suffering and difficulty.

Warren Wiersbe

Battles are won in the trenches, in the grit and grime of courageous determination; they are won day by day in the arena of life.

Charles Swindoll

Failure is one of life's most powerful teachers. How we handle our failures determines whether we're going to simply "get by" in life or "press on."

Beth Moore

QUESTION 82

What does the Bible teach us about praising God?

THE QUICK ANSWER

Praise Him! One of the main reasons you go to church is to praise God. But, you need not wait until Sunday rolls around to thank your Heavenly Father. Instead, you can praise Him many times each day by saying silent prayers that only He can hear.

Praise Him

I will praise You with my whole heart.
Psalm 138:1 NKJV

If you're like most folks on the planet, you're busy . . . very busy. At times, you may feel like there simply aren't enough hours in the day to get everything done. And when the demands of life leave you rushing from place to place with scarcely a moment to spare, you may not take time to praise your Creator. But if you forget to praise God—if you forget to praise Him for who He is and what He's done for you—you're making a big mistake.

The Bible makes it clear: it pays to praise God. In fact, worship and praise should be a part of everything you do.

Otherwise, you quickly lose perspective as you fall prey to the demands of everyday life.

Do you really want to know God in a more meaningful way? Then praise Him. And please don't wait until Sunday morning—praise Him all day long, every day, for as long as you live . . . and then for all eternity.

Words fail to express my love for this holy Book, my gratitude for its author, for His love and goodness. How shall I thank him for it?

Lottie Moon

A child of God should be a visible beatitude for joy and a living doxology for gratitude.

C. H. Spurgeon

Praise reestablishes the proper chain of command; we recognize that the King is on the throne and that he has saved his people.

Max Lucado

Nothing we do is more powerful or more life-changing than praising God.

Stormie Omartian

What does the Bible say about prayer?

THE QUICK ANSWER

Pray early and often: One way to make sure that your heart is in tune with God is to pray often. The more you talk to God, the more He will talk to you.

Too Busy to Pray?

And everything—whatever you ask in prayer,
believing—you will receive.
Matthew 21:22 HCSB

In case you've been wondering, wonder no more—God does answer your prayers. What God does not do is this: He does not always answer your prayers as soon as you might like, and He does not always answer your prayers by saying "Yes."

God isn't an order-taker, and He's not some sort of cosmic vending machine. Sometimes—even when we want something very badly—our loving Heavenly Father responds to our requests by saying "No," and we must accept His answer, even if we don't understand it.

God answers prayers not only according to our wishes but also according to His master plan. We cannot know that plan, but we can know the Planner . . . and we must trust His wisdom, His righteousness, and His love.

Of this you can be sure: God is listening, and He wants to hear from you now. So what are you waiting for?

A life growing in its purity and devotion will be a more prayerful life.

E. M. Bounds

God knows that we, with our limited vision, don't even know that for which we should pray. When we entrust our requests to him, we trust him to honor our prayers with holy judgment.

Max Lucado

Prayer guards hearts and minds and causes God to bring peace out of chaos.

Beth Moore

Two wings are necessary to lift our souls toward God: prayer and praise. Prayer asks. Praise accepts the answer.

Mrs. Charles E. Cowman

Find a place to pray where no one imagines that you are praying. Then, shut the door and talk to God.

Oswald Chambers

It's hard to keep my priorities straight. What does the Bible say about priorities?

THE QUICK ANSWER

Unless you put first things first, you're bound to finish last. And don't forget that putting first things first means God first.

The Right Priorities

The thing you should want most is God's kingdom and doing what God wants. Then all these other things you need will be given to you.
Matthew 6:33 NCV

Sure you're a busy person, and sure you've lots of things to do, but remember this: everything on your to-do list is not created equal. Certain tasks are extremely important while others are not. Therefore, it's important you prioritize your daily activities and complete each task in the approximate order of its importance.

The principle of doing first things first is simple in theory but more complicated in practice. Well-meaning family, friends, and coworkers have a way of making unexpected demands upon your time. Furthermore, each day has it own share of minor emergencies; these urgent matters tend to draw your attention away from more important ones. On paper, prioritizing is simple, but to act upon those priorities in the real world requires maturity, patience, determination, and balance.

If you fail to prioritize your day, life will automatically do the job for you. So your choice is simple: prioritize or be prioritized. It's a choice that will help determine the quality of your life.

Are you living a balanced life that allows time for worship, for family, for school, for exercise, and a little time left over for you? Or do you feel overworked, under-appreciated, and overwhelmed? If your to-do list is "maxed out" and your energy is on the wane, it's time to restore a sense of balance to your life. You can do so by turning the concerns and the priorities of this day over to God—prayerfully, earnestly, and often. Then, you must listen for His answer . . . and trust the answer He gives.

The essence of the Christian life is Jesus: that in all things He might have the preeminence, not that in some things He might have a place.

Franklin Graham

Sin is largely a matter of mistaken priorities. Any sin in us that is cherished, hidden, and not confessed will cut the nerve center of our faith.

Catherine Marshall

Everybody (including me) has problems. What can God's Word teach about my problems?

THE QUICK ANSWER

When it comes to solving problems, work beats worry. Remember: It is better to fix than to fret.

Problem-Solving 101

Consider it a sheer gift, friends, when tests and challenges come
at you from all sides. You know that under pressure,
your faith-life is forced into the open and shows its true colors.
So don't try to get out of anything prematurely.
Let it do its work so you become mature
and well-developed, not deficient in any way.
James 1:2-4 MSG

Here's a riddle: What is it that is too unimportant to pray about yet too big for God to handle? The answer, of course, is: "nothing." Yet sometimes, when the challenges of the day seem overwhelming, we may spend more time worrying about our troubles than praying about them. And, we may spend more time fretting about our problems than solving them. A far better strategy, of course, is to pray as if everything depended entirely upon God and to work as if everything depended entirely upon us.

When we learn to see our problems as God sees them—as opportunities for transformation and growth—we begin to change our lives and our world. And the best day to begin that transformation is the present one.

Often, in the midst of great problems, we stop short of the real blessing God has for us, which is a fresh vision of who He is.

Anne Graham Lotz

Winners see an answer for every problem; losers see a problem in every answer.

Barbara Johnson

Life will be made or broken at the place where we meet and deal with obstacles.

E. Stanley Jones

Faith does not eliminate problems. Faith keeps you in a trusting relationship with God in the midst of your problems.

Henry Blackaby

The size of a person is more important than the size of the problem.

John Maxwell

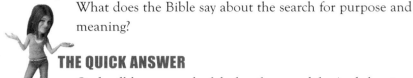

What does the Bible say about the search for purpose and meaning?

THE QUICK ANSWER

God still has a wonderful plan for your life. And the time to start looking for that plan—and living it—is now.

The Search for Purpose

We know that all things work together for the good of those who love God: those who are called according to His purpose.
Romans 8:28 HCSB

"What on earth does God intend for me to do with my life?" It's an easy question to ask but, for many of us, a difficult question to answer. Why? Because God's purposes aren't always clear to us. Sometimes we wander aimlessly in a wilderness of our own making. And sometimes, we struggle mightily against God in an unsuccessful attempt to find success and happiness through our own means, not His.

Are you genuinely trying to figure out God's purpose for your life? If so, you can be sure that with God's help, you will eventually discover it. So keep praying, and keep watching. And while you're at it, guard your steps by making sure that you're obeying all of God's rules, not just the ones that are easy or convenient. When you do these things, you can rest assured that God will eventually make His plans known to you—and you'll be eternally grateful that He did.

In the very place where God has put us, whatever its limitations, whatever kind of work it may be, we may indeed serve the Lord Christ.

Elisabeth Elliot

How much of our lives are, well, so daily. How often our hours are filled with the mundane, seemingly unimportant things that have to be done, whether at home or work. These very "daily" tasks could become a celebration of praise. "It is through consecration," someone has said, "that drudgery is made divine."

Gigi Graham Tchividjian

When God speaks to you through the Bible, prayer, circumstances, the church, or in some other way, he has a purpose in mind for your life.

Henry Blackaby and Claude King

Without God, life has no purpose, and without purpose, life has no meaning.

Rick Warren

QUESTION 87

What does the Bible say about sadness and sorrow?

THE QUICK ANSWER

The thought of a sovereign and loving God will help dispel the inevitable sadness you'll experience from time to time.

When You're Sad

Why are you cast down, O my soul? And why are you disquieted within me? Hope in God; For I shall yet praise Him, The help of my countenance and my God.
Psalm 42:11 NKJV

Sometimes, you feel happy, and sometimes you don't. When you're feeling sad, here are two very important things you should do: 1. Talk to your parents about your feelings. 2. Talk to God about your feelings.

Talking with your parents is helpful because your mom and dad understand this: The problems that seem VERY BIG to you today probably won't seem so big tomorrow.

Talking with God helps because God hears your prayers and He helps make things better.

So the next time you're sad, don't hold your feelings inside—talk things over with your parents and with God. When you do, you'll feel better . . . and so will they!

When we cry, we allow our bodies to function according to God's design—and we embrace one of the "perks" he offers to relieve our stress.

Barbara Johnson

God is good, and heaven is forever. These two facts should brighten up even the darkest day.

Marie T. Freeman

I am sure it is never sadness—a proper, straight, natural response to loss—that does people harm, but all the other things, all the resentment, dismay, doubt, and self-pity with which it is usually complicated.

C. S. Lewis

No more imperfect thoughts. No more sad memories. No more ignorance. My redeemed body will have a redeemed mind. Grant me a foretaste of that perfect mind as you mirror your thoughts in me today.

Joni Eareckson Tada

Music puts to flight all sad thoughts.

Martin Luther

I can be very hard on myself at times. What does the Bible say about my self-worth?

THE QUICK ANSWER

Don't worry too much about self-worth: Instead, worry more about living a life that is pleasing to God. Learn to think optimistically. Find a worthy purpose. Find people to love and people to serve. When you do, your self-worth will, on most days, take care of itself.

What You're Worth

God began doing a good work in you, and I am sure he will continue it until it is finished when Jesus Christ comes again.
Philippians 1:6 NCV

How many people in the world are exactly like you? The only person in the world who's exactly like you . . . IS YOU! And that means you're special: special to God, special to your family, special to your friends, and a special addition to God's wonderful world!

But sometimes, when you tired, angry, dejected, or depressed, you may not feel very special. In fact, you may decide that you're the ugliest duckling in the pond, a not-very-special person . . . but whenever you think like that, you're mistaken.

The Bible says that God made you in "an amazing and wonderful way." So the next time that you start feeling like you don't measure up, remember this: when God made all the people of the earth, He only made one you. You're incredibly valuable to God, and that means that you should think of yourself as a V.I.P. (Very Important Person). God wants you to have the best, and you deserve the best . . . you're worth it!

You are valuable just because you exist. Not because of what you do or what you have done, but simply because you are.

Max Lucado

If you ever put a price tag on yourself, it would have to read "Jesus" because that is what God paid to save you.

Josh McDowell

Being loved by Him whose opinion matters most gives us the security to risk loving, too—even loving ourselves.

Gloria Gaither

Find satisfaction in him who made you, and only then find satisfaction in yourself as part of his creation.

St. Augustine

Sometimes I say things that I shouldn't say. What does the Bible teach me about the way that I should talk to other people?

THE QUICK ANSWER

Words, words, words . . . are important, important, important! So make sure that you think first and speak next. Otherwise, you may give the greatest speech you wish you'd never made!

Watch Your Words

For the one who wants to love life and to see good days must keep his tongue from evil and his lips from speaking deceit.
1 Peter 3:10 HCSB

Okay, how can you guard your heart? A great place to start is by guarding your words. And make no mistake—you'll feel better about yourself if you pay careful attention to the things you say.

Of course you must never take the Lord's name in vain, but it doesn't stop there. You must also try to speak words of encouragement, words that lift others up, words that give honor to your Heavenly Father.

When you're frustrated or tired, you may say things that would be better left unsaid. And whenever you lash out in anger, you miss a wonderful opportunity—the opportunity to consider your thoughts before you speak them.

A far better strategy, of course, is to do the more difficult thing: to think first and to speak next. When you do, you give yourself more time to compose your thoughts and to consult your Creator (but not necessarily in that order!).

The Bible warns that you will be judged by the words you speak (Matthew 12:36-37). And, Ephesians 4:29 instructs you to make "each word a gift" (MSG). These passages make it clear that God cares very much about the things you say and the way you say them. And if God cares that much, so should you.

The great test of a man's character is his tongue.

Oswald Chambers

Change the heart, and you change the speech.

Warren Wiersbe

A little kindly advice is better than a great deal of scolding.

Fanny Crosby

Attitude and the spirit in which we communicate are as important as the words we say.

Charles Stanley

When it comes to my faith, I want to keep growing. How can I do that?

THE QUICK ANSWER

Spiritual maturity is a journey, not a destination.

Your Spiritual Journey

Run away from infantile indulgence. Run after mature righteousness—faith, love, peace—joining those who are in honest and serious prayer before God.
2 Timothy 2:22 MSG

When will you be a "fully-grown" Christian? Hopefully never—or at least not until you arrive in heaven! As a believer living here on planet earth, you're never "fully grown"; you always have the potential to keep growing.

In those quiet moments when you open your heart to God, the One who made you keeps remaking you. He gives you direction, perspective, wisdom, and courage.

Would you like a time-tested formula for spiritual growth? Here it is: keep studying God's Word, keep obeying His commandments, keep praying (and listening for answers), and keep trying to live in the center of God's will. When you do, you'll never stay stuck for long. You will, instead, be a growing Christian . . . and that's precisely the kind of Christian God wants you to be.

If all struggles and sufferings were eliminated, the spirit would no more reach maturity than would the child.

Elisabeth Elliot

Growth takes place in quietness, in hidden ways, in silence and solitude. The process is not accessible to observation.

Eugene Peterson

God does not discipline us to subdue us, but to condition us for a life of usefulness and blessedness.

Billy Graham

We have tasted "that the Lord is good" (Psalm 34:8), but we don't yet know how good he is. We only know that his sweetness makes us long for more.

C. H. Spurgeon

The vigor of our spiritual lives will be in exact proportion to the place held by the Bible in our lives and in our thoughts.

George Mueller

Sometimes I feel like my strength is almost gone. What can I do about that?

THE QUICK ANSWER

Need strength? Let God's Spirit reign over your heart. Anne Graham Lotz writes, "The amount of power you experience to live a victorious, triumphant Christian life is directly proportional to the freedom you give the Spirit to be Lord of your life!" And remember that the best time to begin living triumphantly is the present moment.

Need Strength?

Be of good courage, and let us be strong for our people and for the cities of our God. And may the Lord do what is good in His sight.
1 Chronicles 19:13 NKJV

God is a never-ending source of strength and courage when we call upon Him. When we are weary, He gives us strength. When we see no hope, God reminds us of His promises. When we grieve, God wipes away our tears.

Do you feel burdened by today's responsibilities? Do you feel pressured by the ever-increasing demands of 21st-century life? Then turn your concerns and your prayers over to God. He knows your needs, and He has promised to meet those needs. Whatever your circumstances, God will protect you and care for you if you allow Him to preside over your life.

Today, invite God into your heart and allow Him to renew your spirits. When you trust Him and Him alone, He will never fail you.

Life can be challenging, but fear not. God loves you, and He will protect you. Whatever your challenge, God can handle it. Let Him.

No matter how heavy the burden, daily strength is given, so I expect we need not give ourselves any concern as to what the outcome will be. We must simply go forward.

Annie Armstrong

God conquers only what we yield to Him. Yet, when He does, and when our surrender is complete, He fills us with a new strength that we could never have known by ourselves. His conquest is our victory!

Shirley Dobson

If we take God's program, we can have God's power—not otherwise.

E. Stanley Jones

What does the Bible say about success?

THE QUICK ANSWER

Don't let others define success for you. That's between you and God.

Your Success

The one who acquires good sense loves himself;
one who safeguards understanding finds success.
Proverbs 19:8 HCSB

Do you believe that God has a wonderful plan for your life . . . and do you believe that you can discover that plan and attain it? You should because God has marvelous things in store for you.

When it comes to the important things in life, promise yourself that you won't settle for second best. And what, pray tell, are the "important things"? Your faith, your family, your health, and your relationships, for starters. In each of these areas, you can—and should—be a rip-roaring, top-drawer success.

So, if you want to achieve the best that life has to offer, convince yourself that you have the ability to earn the rewards you desire. Become sold on yourself—sold on your opportunities, sold on your abilities, sold on God's faithfulness to you and yours. If you're sold on yourself, chances are the world will soon become sold, too, and the results will be beautiful.

Success in any field is costly, but the man who will pay the price can have it. The laws of success operate also in the higher field of the soul—spiritual greatness has its price.

A. W. Tozer

Winners see an answer for every problem; losers see a problem in every answer.

Barbara Johnson

The ability to be holy and powerful and effective is to take that which is inevitable, that which is sure, that which is the promise of God, and bank our lives on it.

Franklin Graham

In essence, my testimony is that there is life after failure: abundant, effective, spirit-filled life for those who are willing to repent hard and work hard.

Beth Moore

God has given me special talents and unique opportunities. What should I do with my talents?

THE QUICK ANSWER

Each person possesses special abilities that can be nurtured carefully or ignored totally. The challenge, of course, is to do the former and to avoid the latter.

Using Your Talents

According to the grace given to us, we have different gifts: If prophecy, use it according to the standard of faith; if service, in service; if teaching, in teaching; if exhorting, in exhortation; giving, with generosity; leading, with diligence; showing mercy, with cheerfulness.
Romans 12:6-8 HCSB

God knew precisely what He was doing when He gave you a unique set of talents and opportunities. And now, God wants you to use those talents for the glory of His kingdom. So here's the $64,000 question: are you going to use those talents, or not?

Our Heavenly Father instructs us to be faithful stewards of the gifts that He bestows upon us. But we live in a world that encourages us to do otherwise. Ours is a society that is filled to the brim with countless opportunities to squander our time, our resources, and our talents. So we must be watchful for distractions and temptations that might lead us astray.

If you're sincerely interested in building a successful career, build it upon the talents that God (in His infinite wisdom) has given you. Don't try to build a career around the talents you wish He had given you.

God has blessed you with unique opportunities to serve Him, and He has given you every tool that you need to do so. Today, accept this challenge: value the talent that God has given you, nourish it, make it grow, and share it with the world. After all, the best way to say "Thank You" for God's gifts is to use them.

Not everyone possesses boundless energy or a conspicuous talent. We are not equally blessed with great intellect or physical beauty or emotional strength. But we have all been given the same ability to be faithful.

Gigi Graham Tchividjian

The Lord has abundantly blessed me all of my life. I'm not trying to pay Him back for all of His wonderful gifts; I just realize that He gave them to me to give away.

Lisa Whelchel

This world is filled with temptations. What should I do?

THE QUICK ANSWER

At every turn in the road, or so it seems, somebody is trying to tempt you with something. Your job is to steer clear of temptation . . . and to keep steering clear as long as you live.

Resisting Temptation

Be sober! Be on the alert! Your adversary the Devil is prowling around like a roaring lion, looking for anyone he can devour.
1 Peter 5:8 HCSB

If you feel like you're being boxed in by temptations, remember this: you're never completely trapped—there's always an escape hatch. And how, you ask, can you find the way out? Well, you can start by talking to God.

Beth Moore observed, "Because Christ has faced our every temptation without sin, we never face a temptation that has no door of escape." Her words apply to you.

So the next time you face a strong urge to do something wrong, slow yourself down and have a little chat with your Creator. When you talk to Him—sincerely, prayerfully, and as often as necessary—you can overcome any temptation. No exceptions.

The only power the devil has is in getting people to believe his lies. If they don't believe his lies, he is powerless to get his work done.

Stormie Omartian

It is easier to stay out of temptation than to get out of it.

Rick Warren

In the worst temptations nothing can help us but faith that God's Son has put on flesh, sits at the right hand of the Father, and prays for us. There is no mightier comfort.

Martin Luther

Our battles are first won or lost in the secret places of our will in God's presence, never in full view of the world.

Oswald Chambers

It is easier to stay out of temptation than to get out of it.

Rick Warren

What does the Bible say about the need to share my faith with others?

THE QUICK ANSWER

D. L. Moody, the famed evangelist from Chicago, said, "Remember, a small light will do a great deal when it is in a very dark place. Put one little tallow candle in the middle of a large hall, and it will give a great deal of light." Make certain that your candle is always lit. Give your testimony, and trust God to do the rest.

Your Testimony

The following night, the Lord stood by him and said, "Have courage! For as you have testified about Me in Jerusalem, so you must also testify in Rome."
Acts 23:11 HCSB

Genuine faith was never meant to be locked up in the heart of a believer—to the contrary, it is meant to be shared with the world. But, if you sincerely wish to share your faith, you must first find it.

How can you find and strengthen your faith? Through praise, through worship, through fellowship, through Bible study, and through prayer. When you do these things, your faith will become stronger, and you will find ways to share your beliefs with your family, with your friends, with your dates, and with the world. And when you do, everybody wins.

Although our actions have nothing to do with gaining our own salvation, they might be used by God to save somebody else! What we do really matters, and it can affect the eternities of people we care about.

Bill Hybels

God has ordained that others may see the reality of His presence by the illumination our lives shed forth.

Beth Moore

If I can love folks the way they are, we have greater chance of winning them to the kingdom.

Dennis Swanberg

Choose Jesus Christ! Deny yourself, take up the Cross, and follow Him—for the world must be shown. The world must see, in us, a discernible, visible, startling difference.

Elisabeth Elliot

I have so much to be thankful for. What should I do?

THE QUICK ANSWER

Don't overlook God's gifts: Every sunrise represents yet another beautifully wrapped gift from God. Unwrap it; treasure it; use it; and give thanks to the Giver.

Saying "Thanks" to God

Thanks be to God for His indescribable gift!
2 Corinthians 9:15 NKJV

Are you basically a thankful person? Do you appreciate the stuff you've got and the life that you're privileged to live? You most certainly should be thankful. After all, when you stop to think about it, God has given you more blessings than you can count. So the question of the day is this: will you slow down long enough to thank your Heavenly Father . . . or not?

Sometimes, life here on earth can be complicated, demanding, and frustrating. When the demands of life leave you rushing from place to place with scarcely a moment to spare, you may fail to pause and thank your Creator for the countless blessings He has given you. Failing to thank God is understandable . . . but it's wrong.

God's Word makes it clear: a wise heart is a thankful heart. Period. Your Heavenly Father has blessed you beyond measure, and you owe Him everything, including your thanks. God is always listening—are you willing to say thanks? It's up to you, and the next move is yours.

The act of thanksgiving is a demonstration of the fact that you are going to trust and believe God.

Kay Arthur

Thanksgiving or complaining—these words express two contrastive attitudes of the souls of God's children in regard to His dealings with them. The soul that gives thanks can find comfort in everything; the soul that complains can find comfort in nothing.

Hannah Whitall Smith

A child of God should be a visible beatitude for joy and a living doxology for gratitude.

C. H. Spurgeon

The ability to rejoice in any situation is a sign of spiritual maturity.

Billy Graham

QUESTION 97

How does the Bible instruct me to direct my thoughts?

THE QUICK ANSWER

Watch what you think. If your inner voice is, in reality, your inner critic, you need to tone down the criticism now. And while you're at it, train yourself to begin thinking thoughts that are more rational, more accepting, and less judgmental.

The Direction of Your Thoughts

Those who are pure in their thinking are happy, because they will be with God.
Matthew 5:8 NCV

Here's something to think about: if you want to guard your heart, you must also guard your thoughts. Why? Because thoughts are intensely powerful things. Your thoughts have the power to lift you up or drag you down; they have the power to energize you or deplete you, to inspire you to greater accomplishments or to make those accomplishments impossible.

The Bible teaches you to guard your thoughts against things that are hurtful or wrong, yet sometimes you'll be tempted to let your thoughts run wild, especially if those thoughts are of the negative variety.

If you've acquired the habit of thinking constructively about yourself and your circumstances, congratulations. But if you're mired in the mental quicksand of negativity—or if your mind has been hijacked by all those false messages that the world keeps pumping out—it's now time to change your thoughts, and by doing so, your life.

———————————

The things we think are the things that feed our souls. If we think on pure and lovely things, we shall grow pure and lovely like them; and the converse is equally true.

Hannah Whitall Smith

No matter how little we can change about our circumstances, we always have a choice about our attitude toward the situation.

Vonette Bright

Whether we think of, or speak to, God, whether we act or suffer for him, all is prayer when we have no other object than his love and the desire of pleasing him.

John Wesley

Sometimes, it's tempting to avoid my responsibilities. What should I do?

THE QUICK ANSWER

Goofing off is contagious. That's why it's important for you to hang out with people who are interested in getting the job done right—and getting it done right now!

Getting the Work Done

But one thing I do: Forgetting what is behind and straining toward what is ahead, I press on toward the goal to win the prize for which God has called me heavenward in Christ Jesus.
Philippians 3:13-14 NIV

Want to become a more responsible person? You can start by doing your work, by doing it promptly, and by doing it well.

God has created a world in which hard work is rewarded and sloppy work is not. Yet sometimes, you may be tempted to seek ease over excellence, or you may be tempted to take shortcuts when God intends that you walk the straight and narrow path.

Today, do the right thing: do your work. Wherever you find yourself—whether at work, home, school, or anyplace in between—give it your best. When you do, you will most certainly win the recognition of your peers. But more importantly, God will bless your efforts and use you in ways that only He can understand. So do your work with focus and dedication. And leave the rest up to God.

The world does not consider labor a blessing, therefore it flees and hates it, but the pious who fear the Lord labor with a ready and cheerful heart, for they know God's command, and they acknowledge His calling.

Martin Luther

Ordinary work, which is what most of us do most of the time, is ordained by God every bit as much as is the extraordinary.

Elisabeth Elliot

Thank God every morning when you get up that you have something which must be done, whether you like it or not. Work breeds a hundred virtues that idleness never knows.

Charles Kingsley

It may be that the day of judgment will dawn tomorrow; in that case, we shall gladly stop working for a better tomorrow. But not before.

Dietrich Bonhoeffer

QUESTION 99

When I'm overcome by worries, what should I do . . . and where should I turn?

THE QUICK ANSWER

Categorize your worries: Carefully divide your areas of concern into two categories: those things you can control and those you cannot control. Once you've done so, spend your time working to resolve the things you can control, and entrust everything else to God.

Beyond Worry

Jesus said, "Don't let your hearts be troubled.
Trust in God, and trust in me."
John 14:1 NCV

When we're worried, there are two places we should take our concerns: to the people who love us and to God.

When troubles arise, it helps to talk about them with parents, grandparents, concerned adults, and trusted friends. But we shouldn't stop there: we should also talk to God through our prayers.

If you're worried about something, pray about it. Remember that God is always listening, and He always wants to hear from you.

So when you're upset about something, try this simple plan: talk and pray. Talk openly to the people who love you, and pray to the Heavenly Father who made you. The more you talk and the more you pray, the better you'll feel.

Worry is the senseless process of cluttering up tomorrow's opportunities with leftover problems from today.

Barbara Johnson

God is bigger than your problems. Whatever worries press upon you today, put them in God's hands and leave them there.

Billy Graham

We are not called to be burden-bearers, but cross-bearers and light-bearers. We must cast our burdens on the Lord.

Corrie ten Boom

This life of faith, then, consists in just this—being a child in the Father's house. Let the ways of childish confidence and freedom from care, which so please you and win your heart when you observe your own little ones, teach you what you should be in your attitude toward God.

Hannah Whitall Smith

Pray, and let God worry.

Martin Luther

What does the Bible teach us about worship?

THE QUICK ANSWER
The best way to worship God is to worship Him sincerely and often.

Worship Him!

Worship the Lord your God and . . . serve Him only.
Matthew 4:10 HCSB

A good way to love yourself more is to worship with people who love and respect you. That's one reason (but certainly not the only reason) that you should be an active member of a supportive congregation.

Every believer—including you—needs to be part of a community of faith. Your association with fellow Christians should be uplifting, enlightening, encouraging, and consistent.

Are you an active member of your fellowship? Are you a builder of bridges inside the four walls of your church and outside it? Do you contribute your time and your talents to a close-knit band of hope-filled believers? Hopefully so. The fellowship of believers is intended to be a powerful tool for spreading God's Good News and uplifting His children. God intends for you to be a fully contributing member of that fellowship. Your intentions should be the same.

I am of the opinion that we should not be concerned about working for God until we have learned the meaning and delight of worshipping Him.

A. W. Tozer

To worship Him in truth means to worship Him honestly, without hypocrisy, standing open and transparent before Him.

Anne Graham Lotz

Each time, before you intercede, be quiet first and worship God in His glory. Think of what He can do and how He delights to hear the prayers of His redeemed people. Think of your place and privilege in Christ, and expect great things!

Andrew Murray

Worship is spiritual. Our worship must be more than just outward expression; it must also take place in our spirits.

Franklin Graham

Serve him completely and willingly,
because the Lord knows
what is in everyone's mind.
He understands everything you think.
If you go to him for help,
you will get an answer.

—

1 Chronicles 28:9 NCV